The Only
is Ethics

Part 1: Sex and Marriage

Sean Doherty

Authentic

21 20 19 18 17 16 15   7 6 5 4 3 2 1

First published 2015 by Authentic Media Limited,
52 Presley Way, Crownhill, Milton Keynes, MK8 0ES.
authenticmedia.co.uk

British Library Cataloguing in Publication Data
A catalogue record for this book is available from the British Library.
ISBN 978-1-78078-144-0

Cover design by Sara Garcia
The chapters included in this work 'Living Out My Story', 'QUILTBAG', 'Sexual Singleness'
and 'As Long as You Love Me', are published individually, all copyright © 2015 by
Sean Doherty.

Living Out My Story
ISBN 978-1-78078-147-1   978-1-78078-436-6 (e-book)

QUILTBAG

ISBN 978-1-78078-146-4   978-1-78078-435-9 (e-book)

Sexual Singleness

ISBN 978-1-78078-148-8   978-1-78078-437-3 (e-book)

As Long as You Love Me

ISBN 978-1-78078-149-5   978-1-78078-438-0 (e-book)

CONTENTS

Living Out My Story

And some pastoral and missional thoughts
about homosexuality along the way

I became a Christian in my mid-teens. Not long afterwards, I came to recognise that I was gay.[1] Of course, today we are used to hearing that sexuality is a spectrum. Many people are in between the homosexual and heterosexual poles. But in my case, at least, my sexual attractions were firmly and exclusively oriented towards other men. At the time, identifying myself as gay was just a simple and natural description of who I was and how I felt.

So, homosexuality is not at all a theoretical issue for me (not that it is for anyone). It is a journey I have walked, mostly joyfully, occasionally painfully, always knowing that God was present within it. I want to tell you my story first, so I have saved the theological and biblical stuff for later. That means some of the things I say now will assume the arguments I set out later (feel free to read ahead if you prefer). But I felt it was important to start with my personal journey.

As a teenager and then a student, I attended evangelical churches which taught and explained what I will call the 'classic' Christian understanding of sex and marriage – namely that sex is a good gift from God but it is a gift that God has given for marriage (and, we must now add, that marriage is between a woman and a man). Not that this view was forced on me – wise and supportive mentors

---

[1] I'll talk later about whether that was the best word to use, but it was the one I used at the time.

encouraged me to read about the subject and to work out what I thought for myself. As a theology undergraduate, I took the opportunity to look at different views and interpretations. I continued to be convinced that sex was indeed a good gift for marriage, and that recent attempts to find exceptions to this were not convincing. To my mind, the classic teaching of the Church about sex was indeed the biblical and authentic Christian one, and so I committed myself to celibacy.

At university, I was open about being gay and celibate amongst Christians and non-Christians alike, and I never experienced homophobic treatment from evangelical Christians – although I was at times scorned or pitied by non-Christians and a few liberal Christians for being celibate. For me, the church was my safe place: far from being ostracised, I was nurtured there, given opportunities to preach, and encouraged to consider whether God might be calling me to ordination. I was a member of the prayer ministry and worship teams of my church, and the exec of my Christian Union (CUs are not normally bastions of radical liberal theological sentiment). The other exec members, who knew about my sexuality, treated me with nothing but respect and affection.

In my experience at least, Christians who believe that same-sex activity was sinful were not homophobic. The issue is what you do, not your orientation. Unconditional love and acceptance of a person does not imply unconditional approval of everything they do. Such love and acceptance was my consistent experience.

Tragically, the church has not always treated gay people so well. Some people have been held back from ministry and even excluded from baptism and communion simply because of their sexual orientation, regardless of whether they were sexually active or not. Some have been insulted and mistreated – whereas the Bible commands us to treat people with 'gentleness and respect' (1 Pet. 3:15).[2]

So there is homophobia in the church, although not necessarily more than in any other context. But in my experience, it is undeniable that there is also love and unconditional acceptance of gay people just as we are. Homophobia is an irrational hatred of gay people based simply on the fact that we are gay. But I experienced no 'irrational hatred', even though I was in an environment which taught that sex was only for marriage between a man and a woman. Indeed, that was what I believed too. And I did not have irrational hatred of myself. Believing that gay sex is not right is not the same as irrationally hating or fearing gay people. Homophobia can coexist with the view that gay sex is wrong, but this view does not cause homophobia. We must confront and challenge real homophobia, and there is enough of that to deal with, without pretending that classic Christian convictions about sexual morality are inherently homophobic.

Single and celibate

So I had accepted myself as gay and decided to be celibate, and in church I had been both accepted for who

---

[2]For example, see Wesley Hill, 'The Church is Homophobic – True or False?' at http://spiritualfriendship.org/2014/01/31/the-church-is-homophobic-true-or-false/.

I was, and supported to live celibately. I never tried to change my sexual orientation, although I did pray a few times that my orientation would change. When it did not, I felt it was right to leave it at that, as in the example of Paul with his 'thorn in the flesh' in 2 Corinthians 12:7–9. Whatever this thorn was (we don't really know – perhaps a chronic physical ailment), Paul asked God 'three times' to take it away. His first assumption was that God would intervene. And I absolutely believe that God can and does at times intervene to bring about miraculous transformation (not just in our sexualities). But in my case there was not (and still has not been) any miraculous change in my feelings. Paul's example was very helpful in teaching me that God can be present in the challenges we face, not just in overcoming them. Indeed, his power is not only present in our weakness but 'made perfect' in it (verse 9).

There were advantages to thinking I would remain single. I didn't have to wonder if there was someone out there for me, or spend time looking for them. I had to face squarely the likelihood that I would not share my life with a specific companion, have sexual intimacy with another person or have children. I could grieve for these things – whereas many single people find the perpetual uncertainty as to whether they will marry or not very hard. Instead, I channelled my attention into living as well as I could as a single person – in particular, cultivating friendships, and growing in my relationship with God.

Singleness inevitably brought challenges too. There were times of loneliness. I have wonderful friends and close family, yet from time to time I especially missed having a 'special someone' who was there just for me. This has led me to believe that (like Jesus and his disciples), everyone needs these kinds of intentional, special friendships with others, even though only marriage should be the place for a sexual relationship.

Occasionally I developed feelings for particular guys that I knew. I was lucky in the sense that I never fell deeply in love with another man, but a couple of times it was hard to realise I had feelings for guys (based on the desire for intimacy and closeness rather than on physical attraction), and to choose not to act on them. I found it easier not to tell them, although others in similar situations have found it more helpful to talk to the person (or at least to someone who knows them both) in order to be accountable and clear the air.

Despite these challenges, on the whole I was pretty peaceful about my sexual orientation, and the prospect of remaining celibate. But you may have heard the joke: 'How do you make God laugh? Tell him your plans.' I assumed that celibacy was the cross I had to bear, that it would be permanent, because sexual orientation is permanent – isn't it? God had surprises in store!

Opening up to God's plans

Looking back now, I would say that I had put God and myself in a box. Because of my orientation, I had made assumptions about what God might and might not do in my life. And I had put myself into a box by assuming that my sexual desires would never change. This led me almost to idolise my celibacy, in the sense that I let it define me.

Over time, God changed a number of things about the way I understood my sexual orientation, and therefore my identity.

First, I realised that it was up to God whether I remained single, not me. By focusing on my orientation, I had drawn my own conclusions about the way life would pan out. But God's purpose in our lives often unfolds gradually. Usually, God does not tell us everything in advance! Whilst much of God's general will for our lives is set out in Scripture, we discover his specific will for our particular callings as individuals, families, churches and so on along life's way. (Of course, that must accord with Scripture.) Focussing on myself, on my orientation, meant I had not waited for God's voice afresh at each stage. Yet I tried to listen to God and discern God's will in other areas of my life. The crucial shift was doing this with my sexuality and celibacy too. I started to be more open and less certain about what God's will would be for that part of my life.

Alongside this was a growing sense that God was actually interested in my sexuality. God cared about it, wanted to work in it. Although it was right to surrender my sexuality to God's will by abstaining from sexual activity, surrender on its own was not sufficient. Whilst there was no guarantee that God would transform my sexual desires, I came to believe that God was able and willing to do so.

As I look back on this stage of my journey, I find the work of psychologist William F. Kraft very illuminating (although I hadn't read it at the time). He argues that many of us assume that the only two ways of handling sexual desire are repression and gratification.[3] But both of these are unhealthy! It is true that there are many times when we should not indulge sexual desire, but this does not mean we must repress it. Kraft argues that we can instead *suppress* it, which means accepting your feelings without choosing to promote or act on them. This was true for me: I had not sought to deny my sexuality. I accepted my orientation and myself but did not act on my desires.

But, Kraft says, even suppression is, ideally, only one stage along a journey towards integration.[4] For me, this meant letting God into my sexuality – even into my unwanted desires, so that God could do what God wanted with them. I already accepted that God loved me just as I was – a central gospel truth. But there is another central gospel truth: whilst God loves us just as we are, God also loves us enough not to leave us that way.

So, here were two key insights: I had to keep listening to God and not assume I would stay on the path I had been expecting; God had the power and desire to bring change (or integration) to my sexuality. But the third and final shift was the most important one.

Identity rather than orientation

The most important shift in the way I saw myself was a change in how I saw my sexual identity. This change took

---

[3]William F. Kraft, *Whole and Holy Sexuality: How to Find Human and Spiritual Integrity as a Sexual Person* (Eugene, OR: Wipf and Stock, 1989), p. 83.

[4]*Whole and Holy Sexuality*, p. 90 onwards.

place in a theology lecture I happened to attend. The lecturer asked the rhetorical question, 'Did God create four sexes?' My brain automatically supplied the answer: no. God did not create straight women, straight men, gay women and gay men. God created two sexes, with the capacity to relate to one another sexually. In other words, I had regarded my sexual orientation as what defined my sexual identity. It determined whether I could get married or not. But the Bible, as the lecturer's words reminded me, defines sexuality in much more earthy, physical and bodily terms: 'male and female he created them' (Gen. 1:27). I realised that my sexual identity was not discerned in my sexual desires but in the plain, tangible fact that I am a man. Thus, as a man, God's original intention for me in creation was to be able to relate sexually to a woman (not that all women and men will be called to relate sexually to someone of the opposite sex). This was still true, even though currently my sexual feelings did not match it. This opened up for me the possibility of marriage.

This takes a bit of explaining in a culture that places such a strong emphasis on being true to our feelings. When constructing our sexual identity, we tend to emphasise our feelings: they define with whom we might or might not form a healthy relationship. I was a typical example of this: having a same-sex *orientation* immediately led to a conclusion about my sexual *identity*. There was no shame in that identity – perhaps because of our general cultural attitude now, or because my parents never regarded homosexuality as problematic. Identifying as gay was a simple acknowledgement of my orientation. But, gradually,

I came to believe that in fact it was my feelings that were relatively superficial, in comparison to my physical identity. It is not that sexual feelings are unimportant according to the Bible, but they should not define us.

What this meant for me was that without denying or ignoring my sexual feelings I stopped regarding them as being who I was, and started regarding my body as defining my sexual identity. I felt God calling me to stop identifying myself as gay – even though at this stage I had not experienced any change in my sexual orientation. When I stopped identifying myself as gay, I *did* experience some change – enough that subsequently I fell in love with and eventually married Gaby, who had been a good friend for several years.

The overall pattern of my sexual desires has not changed. I am still predominantly same-sex attracted. In a sense it has ceased to matter to me whether I am attracted to women or men in general. But it matters a great deal that I am attracted to my wife! Of course, nearly all married people are attracted to other people at times. But marriage is about being attracted and called to be faithful to one person in particular, and our marriage is certainly a happy and fulfilling one. We face our share of challenges, but they are usually things such as tidying the house, juggling work with family commitments, and how grumpy I feel in the mornings, and hardly ever about sex!

Why gay people feel so marginalised by the church

My experience helps explain (although it does not magically solve) the massive pressure inside and outside the church to change our moral teaching to fit contemporary views about same-sex relationships. Since in our culture we tend to define sexual identity by sexual feelings, no wonder lesbian and gay people (as a group) feel marginalised and excluded by the church. Church teaching on sex and marriage means that gay people feel excluded de facto from marriage, many forms of family life, sexual intimacy and so on. If being gay precludes you from marrying someone of the opposite sex, then being gay means no sex, no children of your own, and no intimate companionship.

But my experience shows that it is the combination of Christian teaching on sex with the very recent assumption that your sexual attractions define you which causes this. It is not the conviction that sex is only for (opposite-sex) marriage that causes an injustice but the assumption that some people are inherently excluded from marriage simply by being who they are. In our society now, the presumed solution to the injustice this creates is to dismantle classic Christian sexual morality. But my experience calls into question the idea that some people are inherently excluded from marriage by their sexuality. The dominant view of sexual identity today is an incredibly recent development. If we have to choose between this development and the classic Christian interpretation of Scripture, it is not obvious to me why we should ditch the latter. I found it freeing to doubt contemporary assumptions about sexual identity. This opened new possibilities to me, and enabled me to accept myself more fully as I am, that is, physically. Rather than downplaying the significance of our actual bodies, and far from being anti-body and anti-sex, the traditional Christian view acknowledges the goodness of our bodies as male or female, rather than subordinating them to our sexual orientation when it comes to defining sexual identity.

Mark Yarhouse, whose work we shall look at more closely below, therefore argues that we should distinguish between sexual *attraction* (a general description of feelings), sexual *orientation* (a strong and persistent pattern of sexual feelings), and sexual *identity* (a person's understanding of themselves).[5]

What is real homophobia, and how can we prevent it?

According to Stonewall, homophobia is 'the irrational hatred, intolerance, and fear of lesbian, gay and bisexual people'.[6] That is, homophobia is negative feelings or treatment of someone based purely on our sexuality, rather than because of anything we might do about it. But being gay is no more sinful than being straight. Both orientations involve sexual temptation and attractions to people outside opposite-sex marriage (unless there are a few holy and very unusual people out there who

[5]Mark Yarhouse, *Homosexuality and the Christian* (Bloomington, MN: Bethany House, 2010), pp. 41–2. See also Andrew Goddard and Don Horrocks, *Resources for Church Leaders: Biblical and Pastoral Responses to Homosexuality* (London: Evangelical Alliance, 2012), pp. 25–8.
[6]See 'What is homophobia', online at http://www.stonewall.org.uk/at_home/sexual_orientation_faqs/2697.asp.

have only ever been attracted to their spouse). The reality is that everyone's sexual desires are distorted by sin, and we all need God's forgiveness. So, on the whole it is absolutely essential to treat gay people just like anyone else. Homophobia is treating us differently because of our sexuality.

Let me give you a couple of real examples. A church with a number of attendees who were cohabiting with their (opposite sex) partner did not allow them to take a public leadership role within the church because they were in a sexual relationship outside marriage. They recognised that the Christian view is not that sex is for a man and a woman as such but that it is for opposite-sex marriage. By contrast, another church discovered that one of its male leaders was sleeping with his girlfriend but took no action, yet they did not allow a gay person who was seeking to live a celibate life to be involved in children's ministry. (What makes this even worse is the prejudice that a gay person is also more likely to be a paedophile, whereas of course they are entirely separate.) Whether you agree with these specific boundaries or not, one church was consistent and the other was not. It is homophobic to treat gay or same-sex oriented people differently to the way you treat straight people.

One particularly dangerous form of homophobia is so-called 'jokes' and negative generalisations about gay people. This is deeply damaging, spiritually and psychologically. It can make us feel ashamed of who we are and make it harder for us to believe that God loves us. It certainly makes it harder for us to talk openly about our sexuality and thereby find acceptance and support. One celibate guy I know was on the verge of coming out to his pastor, when his pastor joked about something being 'gay'. He was devastated and no longer felt able to talk to his pastor, isolating him at a time when he most needed encouragement and love. If you are serious about gay people trusting and feeling safe in church, it is crucial to cut out these behaviours from your life, and to challenge them in others, inviting them to repent where appropriate.

Given that many LGBT+ people have been hurt by the church, how can we make sure they feel welcome and accepted?

A friend who is a vicar rang me up to ask for advice: 'Sean, a gay couple have started coming to my church. What should I do?'

I replied, 'Have you tried offering them a cup of tea?'

This reply might seem absurdly simplistic (and I did go on to say more than that). My point was simply that gay people aren't different. We have the same basic human needs as anyone else: to be welcomed warmly and hospitably, to be accepted as we are – and to meet with Jesus. In one important way, we should not think that the situation of LGBT+ people is different to anyone else's, just because of our sexuality.

But because of the way that some LGBT+ people have been treated by the church, and because of the extremely negative media picture of the church with respect to sexuality, many gay people are wary of church and Christianity.

Understandably, they do not want to be hurt too, or hurt again.

If a gay person or couple comes to your church, or if someone comes out to you, in itself that is a fantastic start. They have taken a brave step and placed trust in you. Say that you are glad and grateful that they are there, and that they are welcome just as they are, although don't overdo it or be patronising. Apart from this, be normal. Get to know them, invite them for coffee, do whatever you'd do with anyone else – just basic decent treatment of a fellow human being.

As you get to know them more, ask them how much of their story and journey they want to share with you, and listen. This is always a privilege. If they have been hurt in the past, acknowledge this and take it seriously. Ask them what they would find helpful, or if there is anything you can to do to make things safe and welcoming for them (everyone's different).

I heard a great example of this recently. A gay couple wanted to do an evangelistic course at a church, and they let the church know that they would be coming as a couple. Rather than plunging into chapter and verse about the Bible and sexuality, the pastor invited them for dinner. Without setting aside what he believed, he said that they would be completely welcome. He realised they were taking a brave step, and he asked if there was anything he could do to help ensure they felt welcomed. He asked them to let him know if they encountered any homophobia from other participants on the course. In short, he demonstrated that they already had something to offer and teach him and the wider church.

But doesn't welcoming everyone mean endorsing their beliefs or choices?

God calls the church to welcome everyone, just as God welcomes every one of us 'while we were still sinners' (Romans 5:8). At work, in your neighbourhood, and perhaps in your family, you are already surrounded by people who do not share your beliefs about life, the universe and everything else. Even in church, you will know people with all sorts of different views about politics, ethics and Christian doctrine. Hopefully, you manage to get on with all these people, most of the time.

Imagine that at church you meet a cohabiting (opposite-sex) couple. If you become friends, and especially if one or both of them consider themselves to be Christians, there will come a point for a gentle but honest conversation about how their situation relates to following Christ and his teaching about sex and marriage. But you probably won't plunge into that when you first meet them, nor would it be the sole or dominant topic of your conversation.

It is essential to welcome, love and accept gay people in exactly the same way. They may believe and live differently to you. But there is nothing especially unusual about that. Treating people decently does not mean endorsing everything about them. Rather, welcoming people and treating them with love and respect strengthens the chances that they will meet with God, receive good teaching, and grow in maturity. Precisely by loving and accepting people just as they are, they will see something of God's love for them and surrender their lives more fully to God.

Our model here should be Jesus. He held various moral convictions, yet he responded quite differently to different individuals according to what they needed. Hence, he dramatically challenged the rich young ruler to sell everything, he saved the life of the woman caught in adultery, and told her she was not condemned before telling her not to sin any longer, and he exposed the adulterous hearts of the men who brought the woman to him. Holding our convictions without compromise doesn't mean that we must announce them at every opportunity. It means that we will treat the person in the way that they need so that they can meet with Jesus and be transformed.

If a gay person or same-sex couple start attending a church, their immediate need is almost certainly not to be confronted with the biblical teaching about sex. Of course, sex is something that church leaders should regularly teach on, as part of an ongoing balanced diet of good teaching. But we primarily need to be welcomed warmly, loved and accepted just as we are, and offered a safe environment in which to grow in our faith – precisely to help us live according to biblical teaching.

Should people try to change their sexuality?

There is relatively little evidence either way as to whether efforts to change someone's sexuality through psychotherapy are effective. Certainly, some people who have had this kind of therapy have experienced change – but in the absence of a 'control' group, it is impossible to prove whether or not the therapy caused the change.[7] What we can say for sure (against popular misconceptions) is that there is no sound scientific evidence that they are harmful. Indeed, some evidence suggests that they may benefit some participants, even those whose sexual orientation experiences no change.[8] Mark Yarhouse, part of the team who conducted the most substantial study so far of therapy and sexual orientation change, found that most of the positive benefits reported by people in his research 'were not about a dramatic change in sexual orientation. Rather, participants tended to emphasise their relationship with God, their experience of God's love and acceptance, and spiritual growth. That's not to say that change did not occur.'[9] He therefore believes that therapy is most helpful when the focus is not on changing one particular part of the person's feelings but on assisting them towards greater emotional and spiritual wholeness in general.

Yarhouse believes that the crucial thing to address in therapy is not someone's sexual feelings but their sexual identity – how they see themselves. My experience corroborates this. An important aspect of my journey was coming to believe that a significant part of me, namely my body, was genuinely already oriented towards the

---

[7]Some people experience fluctuations in their sexual attractions quite naturally over the course of their lifetimes, as we will see below.

[8]The best study is Stanton Jones and Mark A. Yarhouse, *Ex-Gays? A Longitudinal Study of Religiously Mediated Change in Sexual Orientation* (Downers Grove, IL: IVP Academic, 2007).

[9]*Homosexuality and the Christian*, p. 94.

possibility of (opposite-sex) marriage. My sexual identity as a man was already fixed and secure. So my primary need was not for my sexual desires to change but to recognise and welcome my existing identity as a good gift from God. The change I then experienced was a result of trusting in the good way God had made me. Rather than changing my feelings, so that I could change my label, I changed my label (or God did) and then my feelings started to follow.

This perspective is important in countering the assumption that straight is somehow normal and gay is not. If a person changes from widespread sexual desire towards people of the same sex to widespread sexual desire towards people of the opposite sex, that is not actually an improvement from a Christian perspective. 'Straight' should not be the goal as such but either fulfilled marriage or fulfilled singleness. So, whilst nobody (least of all people under the age of 18) should be pressurised, still less forced, to have any kind of psychotherapy where these are the goals, I think that people who have made an informed choice to have it should be free to do so.

Should Christians describe themselves as gay, straight, etc?

This touches on the question of whether I and other same-sex oriented Christians should call ourselves gay in the first place. As in my case, the term does not automatically imply an endorsement of same-sex sexual relationships. Similarly, author and theologian Wesley Hill identifies himself as gay but has been prominent in arguing that

Scripture rules out same-sex sexual relationships and advocating celibacy as a fulfilling way of life.[10] He and others, such as Julie Rodgers, have found the term helpful simply to describe their sexual orientation.[11]

Indeed, for me, identifying as gay was actually very helpful for a time, because it meant I was being honest about my orientation. It helped me accept myself as I was, and come to terms with what that meant for my life. These days, as I have said, I prefer not to use the term gay (not least because I am now married with children and it confuses people). This is not because I am ignoring or denying my sexual orientation but because I no longer regard it as the decisive marker of my sexual identity. Biblically speaking, I believe this should be defined in terms of male and female, not heterosexual or homosexual.

This is a point drawn out well by Christian anthropologist Jenell Williams Paris, who argues that the binary concepts of gay and straight can be marginalising and excluding. The term 'straight' is particularly problematic, because it was originally paired with 'bent', a pejorative term for gay people. In each class Paris teaches on sexuality, she therefore 'comes out' as being 'no longer heterosexual'.[12] This is not because she is gay but because 'straight' implies that there is something

---

[10]See Wesley Hill, *Washed and Waiting: Reflections on Christian Faithfulness and Homosexuality* (Grand Rapids, MI: Zondervan, 2010).

[11]See Julie Rodgers, 'Can the Gay be a Good?' online at https://julierodgers.wordpress.com/2014/10/23/can-the-gay-be-a-good/.

[12]Jenell Williams Paris, *The End of Sexual Identity: Why Sex is Too Important to Define Who We Are* (Downers Grove, IL: IVP, 2011), p. 43.

normal about heterosexuality, whereas in a fallen world, every-body's sexuality is equally broken. Sexually desiring many people of the opposite sex to whom you are not married is no better or worse than sexually desiring many people of the same sex. The norm is not straight but marriage or singleness.

It therefore seems preferable to me to eschew words such as gay, straight, homosexual, heterosexual, and so on. I am not sure how accurate these categories are as descriptions of the often complex and fluid nature of sexual desire anyway. But because the term gay itself does not imply a view one way or the other about sexual ethics, there is no absolute reason to avoid it. For some people, it will be helpful pastorally to use the term to describe themselves, whilst others find it more helpful not to define themselves in that way.

Then what about 'ex-gay' or 'healing' homosexuality?

For similar reasons, I would never describe myself as 'ex-gay'. This term makes it sound as if I have experienced more change in my sexual attractions than I really have. It would certainly be very nice if we all stopped experiencing temptation and only desired what was right. But God promises us the power to resist temptation, not to cease experiencing it. Jesus himself experienced temptation in every way that we do.

So, it is not necessary (or possible) to be free here and now of every disordered desire, sexual or otherwise. That will only happen when Jesus returns. Maybe some lucky people experience a total transformation of their sexual desires. I have never met one. But I do have the privilege of knowing many who remain entirely or predominantly same-sex attracted but who believe that their sexual identity is found in the fact that God has made them men or women. Some have become attracted to someone of the opposite sex and gone on to have fulfilling marriages, including sexually. Others, who have not fallen for anyone of the opposite sex, rightly remain single and therefore celibate. But someone who has moved beyond or never adopted the labels of 'gay' and 'straight', who does not define their sexuality in those terms, is not celibate because they are gay but because they are unmarried.

This redresses the profound sense of injustice caused by the perception that the Bible and the church call gay people to be celibate, whilst straight people don't have to be. First, it loosens the perceived connection between celibacy and homosexuality. Some supposedly gay people have normal and fulfilling opposite-sex marriages. Second, being gay isn't what means you should be celibate (as if gay is a special category of person) but rather being single. The playing field is levelled, because all people are called either to celibacy or marriage on the basis of their own particular vocation and situation in life, rather than by virtue of belonging to a particular sexual category.

I never speak of being 'healed' of homosexuality. This language is deeply damaging, because it loads shame onto people at the very deep level of their identity: they may feel told that there is something wrong with the very way that they are. Homosexuality is not an illness or a disease to be cured but rather a disordered desire. Nor is deliverance the answer, since the problem is not a demon. The biblical prescription, for me at least, was truth, the truth that my sexual identity is male, not gay. That was the truth which set me free (John 8:31–32).

Should people who are committed to the mainstream Christian teaching about sex and marriage attend a civil partnership ceremony or same-sex wedding?

This feels like a real catch-22. Assuming that the relationship is sexual (and not intentionally celibate), if you attend a civil partnership ceremony or same-sex wedding, you may feel that you are publicly endorsing the couple's decision to commit themselves to a lifelong sexual relationship which you believe is sinful. And if it's sinful, it's ultimately not best for them.

But if you politely decline to attend the ceremony, the couple (and probably others) will understandably be hurt. They have honoured you by offering you hospitality and inviting you to be part of their special day, especially if they know you are a Christian (most gay people know perfectly well what the usual Christian view is of same-sex relationships). If you don't attend, they may feel personally rejected by you, although you don't mean anything of the sort. You may come across as judgemental and homophobic. Worst of all, this may put some people off the church and therefore off Christ.

So, it seems to be a no-win situation. If you go, you may be sending a message that doesn't truly represent your beliefs. But if you don't go, you may also send a message that doesn't truly represent your beliefs. Whichever you do, you are liable to be misinterpreted.

My wife and I have attended more than one civil partnership ceremony. (We have not yet been invited to any same-sex weddings.) Because we recognised we were potentially going to send the wrong signal whatever we did, we decided that it was more important to show our friends the acceptance and unconditional love that we felt towards them personally, by accepting their offer of hospitality and being present with them. We would prefer people to form a wrong impression of what we think about their sexual ethics, than for them to misunderstand our care for them personally. Attending these ceremonies sought to show them our love and the fact that we valued our friendship.

In one case, neither partner was a practising Christian. Their primary need was to come to know Jesus. Although the gospel always involves repentance as well as faith, we felt that explaining our view of sexual ethics was not the main priority at this stage. Rather, we wanted to send them a strong signal that we care about and support them personally.

In another case, the couple were committed Christians who have reached a different theological view to us about same-sex relationships. They were to have a service of blessing for their relationship immediately following their civil ceremony. In this case, in fear and trembling I rang up one of them and thanked her for the honour of inviting us. I explained that we'd love to come to the civil ceremony but we felt we couldn't be present during the blessing. If it was hurtful or offensive to her (and I knew it could well be) then we would prefer not to come than to hurt them. She was extremely gracious, and encouraged us to come to the civil ceremony and quietly slip out before the blessing. This awkward and potentially hurtful kind of conversation will not always be appropriate, and we need wisdom in working out when to speak, and when to remain silent.

Of course, if somebody sincerely wants to know what you think, then you must give them a gentle but honest answer. But I don't think you should feel guilty or that you are undermining what you believe by attending. You *are* showing them something of your faith, namely that they are precious to God and to you. That is part of the gospel. Of course, the gospel is much more than that, but in the circumstances I think it's more important to show them the aspect of the gospel which they most need at this stage.

What about when someone becomes a Christian?

Our priority must be to accept gay people just as they are. Doing this is not soft-selling the gospel but an expression of it. Jesus accepted people just as they were. But as people met with Jesus, things started to change in their lives. Indeed, it was precisely Jesus's radical acceptance of sinners that transformed them. If a gay person or couple become Christians and start growing in their faith, their lives will change.

But we need to be wary of jumping to conclusions about how people will change and at what speed. We all have many issues in our lives, and God is gracious with us in terms

of accepting us and changing us a bit at a time. God sometimes does stuff immediately. Usually, the process takes time.

One person I know, who was in a long-term same-sex
relationship, became a Christian with his partner through
the ministry of a prayer group. Over time, he felt God
convince him that he needed to break up with his partner
in order to refrain from sex outside marriage.[13] He broke
the news to his partner, and they were both devastated.
The next time he attended the prayer group (his partner
did not attend), he asked for prayer because of the break-
up. The group were astonished. They had not realised
that they were a couple. If they had realised, and confronted them about it, my friend believes that he and his
partner would have run a mile from them, and from God.
Sometimes, God uses our silence. It is the Holy Spirit's job
to convict the world of sin (John 16:8) – not our job.

Another friend and his partner became Christians
and so far have continued to have a sexual relationship.
But God is clearly at work in their lives. Right away, they
fought to give up drugs, and experienced God's help in
that struggle. More recently, my friend has felt God helping him to trust God with his business and financial situation – something many mature Christians still struggle
with. I would obviously love them to lay down their sexual

---

[13] I don't believe that this is the only option for same-sex couples where
one or both partners have become Christians, as I explain here: http://
www.livingout.org/resources/celibate-same-sex-couples, and here: http://
www.livingout.org/resources/becoming-christians-what-if-you-are-an-
ssa-couple.

relationship as they grow in faith. But in the meantime, they are undeniably growing in other ways. And we have been able to have honest conversations without any of us having to change our views of sexual morality.

Of course, if someone exploring faith asks us an honest question about sexual morality, it is important not to bury anything in the small print.[14] When sharing the gospel with someone, it is essential to emphasise that becoming a Christian means taking up your cross to follow Christ, and God turning everything in your life upside down: your money, your career, your relationships. We must not mislead people into thinking that following Jesus means continuing with life in other respects just as before. At the same time, God is patient and may work within different aspects of our lives in different orders and at different times. When people become Christians, we need to give them good teaching, and some space to let God work. This is messy because God doesn't sort everything out overnight – but that is exactly the same with you and me. None of us is the finished article yet either.

What about more mature Christians who are not seeking to live according to biblical teaching?

Christians are called to admonish one another (Col. 3:16). It's quite right to gently encourage one another to follow

---

[14]Sam Allberry, quoted in Justin Brierley, 'A Different Kind of Coming Out' in *Christianity Magazine* (August 2013), online at http://www.premierchristianity.com/Past-Issues/2013/August-2013/A-Different-Kind-of-Coming-Out.

Christ more faithfully, which at times could certainly include directly discussing people's sexual morality with them and exhorting them to conform their lives to Jesus's teaching. But you must not single out Christians in same-sex relationships. It is very important to treat everyone consistently, whether with matters as weighty as baptism and communion, or as trivial as sharing a bedroom at a church weekend away or in your home. Do we do the same with, for example, greedy people, cohabiting couples, and people who gossip?

If you do decide to discuss sexuality with someone directly, it is rarely helpful to go in with all guns blazing. It's probably best to start by asking some open questions, and genuinely listening to what people say. Ask them how much of their story they feel comfortable sharing. Ask them how they relate their sexuality to their faith. Have they explored the current debates in the church for themselves? This will help you to understand how much they have engaged with the classic Christian teaching about sex. Some may never have heard it: knowing that something is generally supposed to be a sin is not at all the same as exploring and understanding the biblical story, its view of sex, and therefore the reasons for its prohibition of same-sex activity. You can help someone in this situation by gently introducing them to this fuller biblical picture, and walking with them as they explore it for themselves – reading, thinking, discussing, and praying.

It is important to be honest about the fact that there is more than one point of view in the church today on this issue – two minutes online and they will discover that for themselves anyway. It's much better to acknowledge this but explain which view you find convincing and why.

Many people have already gone through this process of exploration, and come to a different conclusion on the matter than the one set out here. For me, a helpful question to explore is why they have reached that conclusion. Is it based on an honest engagement with Scripture? That is, what is the real point of difference between you – the interpretation of Scripture or its authority? I often ask people, 'If I could show you that what you believe is not what the Bible says, would you change your mind?' I would indeed change my mind, if someone showed me that my view was not the biblical one. When I ask this question, very often the answer is, 'No.' In other words, the person has not ultimately reached their view on biblical grounds alone.

What about those in church leadership who are not seeking to live according to biblical teaching?

Although I have argued for a very welcoming, accepting approach towards gay people, the New Testament (especially 1 Tim. and Titus) is also clear that those involved in church leadership are called to lead lives in keeping with the church's teaching. Again, it is essential to be consistent and not to prevent some people from entering leadership whilst allowing others whose lives fall equally short. But someone who did not believe in certain core doctrines of the Christian faith would not expect to have a public leadership role in church, such as worship leading, preaching, administering communion and so on. As we will see, the classic Christian view about marriage and sex is not a peripheral, minor aspect of what Christians believe. It is related to and part of the doctrinal core of our faith. How we live is integrally related to what we believe.

Not that you can sort out everything in your life before you get involved in ministry. The key points, with any moral issue, would be for someone to recognise that it is an issue, to repent when they yield to temptation, to desire and seek to live according to Jesus's teaching, and to surrender that aspect of their life to him. That is very different to someone who flatly denies that something is a temptation or issue in the first place. It's not about whether someone already has everything sorted out (none of us do) but about the direction in which they are heading.

Conclusion

I hope that sharing my own journey has demonstrated that the classic Christian teaching about sex is not homophobic – indeed, many same-sex oriented people believe it. Jesus calls us to love and accept everyone unconditionally but to do so without compromising his teaching about sexual ethics. If you want to guide people, you first need to love them. But if you love someone, you will want them to grow in obedience to Christ.

What that looks like will vary from person to person, and will happen at different speeds. Gay people, just like everyone else, need to be assured proactively that we are loved and accepted just as we are. And when it comes to the speed at which our lives change after conversion, we need the same generosity and patience that the church already shows to plenty of other people.

Whether someone experiences any change in their sexual orientation or not, good pastoral care, prayer and in some cases responsible psychotherapy may offer someone a safe space to explore their feelings, accept themselves, and receive support. Fulfilled singleness should be seen as just as successful and legitimate a Christian goal as fulfilled marriage.

Whether someone chooses to identify themselves as gay or not does not automatically imply a view either way about sexual morality. For some people, identifying themselves as gay is an important step of self-acceptance. But the label can become a stumbling block, contributing to the experience of marginalisation and exclusion that many gay people feel. If so, some people may find it liberating to recover their physical sexual identity as their God-given reality, even if in a fallen world their sexual orientation does not fully line up with it. For some people, this change at the level of sexual identity may eventually lead to enough change in sexual feelings that marriage becomes a real possibility.

Opposite-sex-attracted people can help by avoiding labelling themselves as straight or heterosexual. This language reinforces the idea that straight is somehow 'normal' – whereas we are all equally fallen.

However, for most same-sex-attracted people, marriage has not become an option. Here, there is an urgent need for the church to recover and support a much more positive view of singleness as a fulfilling way of life (as I argue in *Sexual Singleness*). So having shown that the classic Christian teaching about marriage and sex has proven to be good and fulfilling in my own life as a gay or same-sex-attracted person, I look in depth at this teaching and the biblical reasons for it in *QUILTBAG: Jesus and Sexuality*, which I invite you to read next.

Go Deeper

True Freedom Trust (http://www.truefreedomtrust.co.uk/)

Andrew Goddard and Don Horrocks (eds.),*Resources for Church Leaders: Biblical and Pastoral Responses to Homosexuality* (London: Evangelical Alliance, 2012).

Wesley Hill, *Washed and Waiting: Reflections on Christian Faithfulness and Homosexuality* (Grand Rapids, MI: Zondervan, 2010).

Ed Shaw, *The Plausibility Problem: The Church and Same-Sex Attraction* (Nottingham: IVP, 2015).

Mark Yarhouse, *Homosexuality and the Christian: A Guide for Parents, Pastors, and Friends* (Bloomington, MN: Bethany House, 2010).

Some articles by Sean on the Living Out website

http://www.livingout.org/resources/how-should-i-respond-if-my-child-comes-out-to-me

http://www.livingout.org/resources/celibate-same-sex-couples

http://www.livingout.org/resources/becoming-christians-what-if-you-are-an-ssa-couple

http://www.livingout.org/is-it-ever-responsible-for-people-with-same-sex-attraction-to-get-married

QUILTBAG

Jesus and sexuality

QUILTBAG – Queer, Undecided, Intersex, Lesbian, Trans-sexual, Bisexual, Asexual, Gay.

What is sexuality?

Terms such as homosexual, heterosexual and bisexual are relatively new. I recently read a book, translated in the mid-1980s, that used the word 'sexuality' to mean that human beings are male and female. Being sexual meant being a physical sex, female or male. Today, 'sexuality' denotes 'sexual orientation' – whether gay, straight, or something else.

Most people today assume that sexuality is something real and definite. You simply are straight, or gay, or bi. Gay people don't choose to be gay any more than straight people choose to be straight. A shorthand for this view is 'essentialism', because it holds that sexuality is an essential part of you. We can even look back through history and identify gay individuals from the past, because we assume that their experience and reality of being gay then is pretty much the same as it is now, though of course far less understood then. The idea that we understand sexuality much better now than in the past massively heightens the pressure on the church to change its view of sexual morality. I have had conversations with people who regard me as blinded by my faith from accepting the 'clear' findings of science concerning sexuality. Our culture tends to assume that it is not our experience of sexuality that is new (people have always been gay, straight, bi and so on), but our improved understanding of it.

I think that essentialism is very simplistic about what 'science' says about sexuality. There has been excellent and insightful research on sexuality, but note two things about that research. First, we need a lot more. There are many things we still don't know, such as what causes sexual orientation. Genetics? Upbringing? A complex mix of different factors?[1] Second, some research actually undermines the essentialist view, suggesting that sexuality is a lot more complicated and diverse than we often assume.[2]

I also think that essentialism is historically simplistic. No doubt there has always been same-sex desire, activity and relationships. But what they have looked like has varied from culture to culture.[3] The ancient writers who wrote

---

[1] See the authoritative recent review of scientific research in this area by Eleanor Whiteway and Denis R. Alexander, 'Understanding the causes of same-sex attraction', in *Science and Christian Belief* (2015), 27, pp. 17–40, online at https://www.scienceandchristianbelief.org/serve_pdf_free.php?filename=SCB+27-1+Whiteway+Alexander.pdf, with additional material here https://www.scienceandchristianbelief.org/download_pdf_free.php?filename=Whiteway-long-version-ed.pdf.

[2] See Peter Ould, 'Can your sexuality change?' online at http://www.livingout.org/can-your-sexuality-change-, and Lisa Diamond, 'Just How Different are Female and Male Sexual Orientation?' a video lecture online at http://www.cornell.edu/video/lisa-diamond-on-sexual-fluidity-of-men-and-women.

[3] See Peter Ould, 'Surely the homosexual activity prohibited by the Bible was totally different to what we're familiar with today?' online at http://www.livingout.org/surely-the-homosexual-activity-prohibited-by-the-bible-was-totally-different-to-what-we-re-familiar-with-today-.

about same-sex relationships in their day were no less sophisticated and observant than us. So, if sexual orientation is universal and an essential part of human identity, I find it surprising that nobody realised this before – that we have an accurate self-knowledge they lacked.

This does not mean that sexual orientation is not real. It is. But it could well be more complicated, varying somewhat in understanding and experience by time and place. The context in which we find ourselves shapes our experience and understanding of ourselves, including our sexualities. So the main rival to essentialism is the theory that sexuality is (at least partly) socially constructed. (This can still include the view that there is something universal underneath the different social constructions, but experienced and understood differently in different cultures.) For example, Professor Sue Wilkinson, who was married (to a man) for seventeen years said, 'I was never unsure about my sexuality throughout my teens or twenties. I was a happy heterosexual and had no doubts. Then I changed, through political activity and feminism, spending time with women's organisations. It opened my mind to the possibility of a lesbian identity.'[4] What was significant for her was involvement in a community in which a new kind of identity became possible. Cultural and social factors may shape sexual identity, at least for some people.

At the radical end of this 'constructed' approach, some people even believe that there is an element of choice involved (although they do not necessarily deny the reality

[4]http://www.wnd.com/2007/07/42356/.

of sexual orientation).[5] Peter Tatchell, who has tirelessly campaigned against the mistreatment of gay people, often at great personal cost, has made some statements that come close to this approach, although he believes that biology is also a factor. For example, he asks, 'If we are all born either gay or straight, how do they explain people who switch in mid-life from fulfilled heterosexuality to fulfilled homosexuality (and vice versa)?'[6]

Similarly, at the more radical end of contemporary gender theory is the idea that we need to deconstruct male and female as fixed, opposite categories, because the very notion of gender is itself corrupt and patriarchal. If male and female do not actually exist as such, how can there be such a thing as sexual orientation?

Almost all of these approaches are onto something. Essentialists best describe how most people today become aware of their sexuality: as a given. Nobody wakes up one day with a completely blank slate and thinks, 'What sexuality shall I be?' Sexual orientation clearly isn't a free choice

---

[5]See http://www.queerbychoice.com/. Similarly, the journalist Matthew Parris has written, 'I think sexuality is a supple as well as subtle thing, and can sometimes be influenced, even promoted; I think that in some people some drives can be discouraged and others encouraged; I think some people can choose.' 'Are you gay or straight? Admit it, you are most likely an in-between.' *The Times* (5.8.2006).

[6]Peter Tatchell, 'Born gay or made gay?' *Guardian* (28.6.2006), online at http://www.theguardian.com/commentisfree/2006/jun/28/borngayor-madegay. See also 'Future Sex: Beyond Gay and Straight', *Huffington Post* (9.1.2012), online at http://www.huffingtonpost.co.uk/peter-g-tatchell/sex-future-beyond-gay-and-straight_b_1195017.html.

in that sense. Indeed, some gay people admit that they would have chosen to be straight if they'd had a choice. It's not that they are ashamed of their sexuality – it's just that life would have been simpler and less painful in a world which is still not fully accepting towards them.

The social constructionists are also onto something in their recognition that society and culture play a major role in making us who we are. When I identified myself as gay, it was simply because that was the word provided for me by my world.

And the more radical 'choice' theorists are also onto something. They are right to recognise that, whilst most people have no choice when it comes to their sexual feelings, adopting a particular sexual identity involves an element of choice – and certainly sexual feelings can be influenced by our choices, although I am not saying that it is possible to change one's sexual orientation through choice.[7] I chose to stop identifying myself as gay, not because I had then experienced any change in my sexual feelings, but because I had come to believe that my sexual identity should be defined in terms of my physical gender and not in terms of my orientation.

As you'll have noticed in what I have just said, homosexuality is a real and personal issue for me. Elsewhere in this series, in *Living Out My Story*, I have shared my story and offered some thoughts about how the church

---

[7]For an excellent if older discussion of choice, see Edward Stein, *The Mismeasure of Desire: The Science, Theory, and Ethics of Sexual Orientation* (New York: Oxford University Press, 1999), ch. 9–10.

can truly welcome and care for gay people, without compromising what I have called the 'classic' Christian view that sex is for marriage only, and that marriage is the union of a woman and a man. In my experience, that conviction was liberating and life-giving. What follows here sets out the theological basis for it.

Understanding why the Bible and the church teach that sex is only for marriage

There has been an inordinate amount of ink spilled over what the various biblical prohibitions of same-sex activity mean. Some authors argue fiercely that these texts refer to sex in a context of idolatry, slavery and paedophilia, and therefore cannot possibly apply to loving, faithful, consenting same-sex relationships today. But these authors have not often engaged with the theological and biblical reasons why the church has classically taught that same-sex activity is prohibited. It is not enough to say that the classic biblical 'proof texts' do not apply to monogamous, faithful same-sex relationships. To be convincing, this perspective needs to show that the reasons for the prohibition no longer apply.

However, an equal weakness amongst those arguing for the classic view, that sex is only for marriage and that marriage is only between a woman and a man, has been a lack of explanation as to why this is so. There's no point keeping a rule unless there are good reasons for it – and many people today can't see the point of this rule, no matter what the texts actually say. Even worse, some proponents of the classic view try to give objectively verifiable reasons for it in order to convince people that it is correct. For example, Christians have claimed that same-sex relationships are inherently less committed or faithful than opposite-sex ones, or that homosexual activity is physically dangerous, that gay people are more likely to develop sexually transmitted diseases, and so on. This approach makes the classic view sound homophobic to contemporary ears, and places itself at the mercy of the next empirical study. You can't use contextual evidence to prove what you are claiming is a universal moral viewpoint. For example, you could equally argue that same-sex relationships have only been less faithful precisely because they did not have the regulation and security of marriage.

So, it should be pretty clear that we need to look at the reasons behind the classic Christian view of sex and marriage, and we turn to this now.

Jesus, sex and marriage

The first and most important reason for the church's teaching is the teaching of Jesus himself. It is sometimes argued that because Jesus never directly mentioned same-sex relationships (or to be precise, that if he did then it is not recorded in the gospels), then the church has no business teaching about them either. But we cannot read too much into Jesus's silence. There are many things the gospels do not mention. They are not intended as an exhaustive rule book.

Given what the Old Testament says about same-sex activity (as we shall see) and the universal disapproval of it within the Judaism of Jesus's time, it would be surprising if Jesus underwent a radical rethink about the issue but never got round to mentioning it. After all, he frequently challenged received wisdom, and the gospels do not shy away from describing the controversies he caused. Jesus's radical love for all and inclusion and acceptance of outcasts did not stop him from saying that sin was sin (as in the famous example of John 8:11).[8]

More concretely, when Jesus was quizzed on a controversial issue of sexual morality within his day (divorce), he looks to the creation stories in Genesis 1 and 2 in order to discern God's intention for marriage and sex. This is why the church has always taken these stories as especially significant. So Jesus is quoting from Genesis when he says, 'God made them male and female' and 'a man shall leave his father and mother and hold fast to his wife, and they shall become one flesh' (Mark 10:7–8, and also Matt. 19:5). Jesus therefore defined and understood marriage as being the union of a woman and a man through sexual intercourse ('one flesh'), precisely because God made human beings female and male. If this was Jesus's view of marriage and the purpose of sex within it, it is difficult to see how we can interpret Jesus as supporting *any* sex outside marriage, including same-sex activity.

If Jesus turned to the creation stories in Genesis 1 and 2 in order to understand marriage and sex, and to resolve a controversial question of sexual morality, that is the best

---

[8]See John Nolland, 'Sexual Ethics and the Jesus of the Gospels', *Anvil* 26.1 (2009), online at http://www.biblicalstudies.org.uk/pdf/anvil/26-1_021.pdf.

model for us to follow also. In our attempt to understand why Scripture prohibits same-sex activity, we will now therefore look at these stories too.

Sexuality and the Trinity

What is the most important thing about God? When I teach on sexuality, I usually start with this question. Someone almost always replies, 'God is love,' to which I answer, 'Why? What makes God love?' That normally elicits silence. Other typical answers are, 'God is the Creator' or 'all-powerful'. All these answers are true, of course, but are they God's most important and fundamental reality? Sooner or later, we hit the answer. Here it is. The most important thing about God is: God is 'Triune'.

Triune is not a word we use regularly, although 'Trinity' is more familiar. Triune shows the original meaning of Trinity: three = one. Most Christians know, in theory at least, that God is somehow both three and one. That's why God is love. At God's deepest level, God is fundamentally relationship – three persons who are different (though equal), but in a relationship of such perfect love that they are one just as much as they are three. God really is three persons, yet there is only one God. Both the oneness and the threeness matter equally.

What has that to do with sex? Well, this relational, tri-personal God says, 'Let us make man in our image, after our likeness' (Gen. 1:26). Note the 'us' and 'our' – as if more than one person is speaking. Many Christian interpreters have read this as a reference to the Trinity, although this was not what it meant originally.[9] But it is striking that when a fundamentally relational God decides to create someone like God, to reflect and represent God in the world, God does it by making us male and female (v. 27).

So, being male and female, being sexual, is how we are like God, because God is fundamentally different persons in fundamental unity. Similarly, women and men are fundamentally different, yet fundamentally the same. Our common humanity unites us, as can the intimacy of sexual intercourse. As Christopher Roberts puts it, 'Marriage relies on two modes of being human that are utterly distinct and yet created for partnership.'[10] It is the genuine difference between women and men which reflects the real difference of persons in God. Yet, just as importantly, men and women are fundamentally the same, reflecting God's own unity. It is only together that we reflect God, and neither gender can reflect God on its own. (This is also why women and men are equal, just as Father, Son and Holy Spirit are equal.)

Following the example of Jesus, the Christian tradition has read these verses as a reference not only to our common humanity, but also to marriage. It would be easy to

---

[9]For fuller discussion of different possible interpretations, see for example Claus Westermann, *Genesis I–II: A Commentary*, trans. John J. Scullion (London: SPCK, 1984), p. 142ff.

[10]Christopher C. Roberts, *Creation and Covenant: The Significance of Sexual Difference in the Moral Theology of Marriage* (London: T & T Clark, 2007), p. 94. The whole book is a must-read if you want to explore this issue more deeply.

assume that only people who are like one another can get along. For example, some ancient writers believed that men could only truly be friends with other men. But in the Trinity, and in Genesis, difference does not hinder union, but enables it. It is precisely the difference between Father and Son which makes their relationship one of perfect fatherhood and sonship. And it is precisely the difference between women and men, including the physical genital difference, that enables them to be truly physically united into 'one flesh' through sexual intercourse (Genesis 2:18). We really can be united, without having to become the same. Indeed, we need to be different, if we are to be united.

Any supporter of same-sex activity from a Christian perspective must therefore answer a fundamental question: how can we regard the union of two people of the same sex as a 'one flesh' union in the sense of Genesis 2? It might well be a 'one heart' and 'one mind' union – but those things alone are not what make a marriage.

In summary, being women and men, i.e. sexually different, is the way humans reflect and are like God. Just as God is relational and interdependent, and not solitary, we too are relational at our most fundamental level. Sex is therefore a permanent, inherent feature of who we are, as we can see in the fact that Jesus's resurrected body is still male. In the new heaven and earth, physical life is not abolished, but reaffirmed and perfected. Therefore sexuality is fundamental to being human, even though having sex is not.[11]

---

[11]*Creation and Covenant*, p. 107.

Marriage and the relationship between Christ and the church

So, the first reason that being sexual creatures matters is that our unity-through-difference reflects God's. The New Testament adds a second reason: marriage is a picture of the gospel. Far from being prudish about marriage and sex, the Bible compares the relationship between God and humanity to sex. Just as wife and husband are fundamentally different, so are Jesus and the church.[12] Yet the wonder of the gospel is that, rather than Jesus remaining separated from the church by his greatness and our sin, he truly unites himself to us, bringing us salvation and wholeness. The gospel is not simply forgiveness (although it is), nor that we have a new relationship with God (although we do). The gospel is also union with Christ: we have been made one with Jesus, and thereby share his holiness and relationship to the Father.

Again, then, the difference between women and men in marriage cannot be downplayed. Our union with Christ doesn't make us the *same* as him. Me is not short for Messiah! Like a married couple, Jesus and his bride remain distinct people. Yet we are utterly made for each other and truly united. This is the reason why sex must be between people who are fundamentally (or ontologically) different to one another, as men and women are fundamentally different. Sex within marriage shows

---

[12]This image is used in Ephesians 5:23–33 and Revelation 19:6–9.

that people who are truly different can also be truly united (which is also why marriage must be a permanent union), and in this way sex is a picture of the gospel.

This means that sex must be between a man and a woman for exactly the same reason that it must be within the permanence of marriage. The point of sex is not simply to unite *any* two individuals, even if they love one another and are completely committed for life, but to embody the union between people who are fundamentally different. The Father, the Son and the Spirit are fundamentally different but perfectly one. Christ and the church are also different, yet truly united. God's good purpose for sex in creation is therefore to show that two fundamentally different people can be permanently and truly united. Anyone who wishes to argue that promiscuity and adultery are wrong but not same-sex activity, needs to show why this fundamental feature of the biblical picture of sex no longer applies, when the other features still do.

Isn't sex within marriage primarily about procreation?

One reason often offered for the classic view of sex advocated here is that procreation can only take place between a woman and a man. This is a very consistent view for Roman Catholics and others who believe that contraception is wrong. For them, sex and procreation cannot be separated. But an overemphasis on procreation is an own goal for people who believe that contraception is legitimate. If sex does not inherently have to be procreative, why restrict it to opposite-sex couples?[13]

It's true that procreation is emphasised in Genesis 1. God blesses humanity and tells them to 'Be fruitful and multiply and fill the earth and subdue it' (v. 28). But this is a general instruction to humanity as a whole, not necessarily an obligation on every married couple. Just as this command does not oblige everyone to marry in the first place, it does not oblige every married couple to procreate. A small minority of couples may choose to remain childless for selfish reasons. But there can also be very good reasons for a couple to remain childless, such as if they are both carriers of a genetic disease or because of mental health concerns. And there are many marriages that are childless through infertility or because they took place after childbearing age. Such marriages are no less valid or good, even without (humanly speaking) the prospect of procreation. Similarly, there are many sexual acts that have the potential for procreation but are not right and natural, such as casual sex, rape and adultery. There is more to marriage than procreation.

Genesis 2 makes no mention of procreation at all. The creation of the woman happens because, as God announces, 'It is not good that the man should be alone' (Gen. 2:18). None of the animals corresponds to the man sexually or in terms of companionship and intimacy. But

---

[13]This is essentially the argument made by Robert Song in *Covenant and Calling: Towards a Theology of Same-Sex Relationships* (London: SCM, 2014).

the woman does, as the man recognises when God presents her to him:

> 'This at last is bone of my bones
> and flesh of my flesh;
> she shall be called Woman,
> for she was taken out of Man.'
> *Genesis 2:23*

This isn't just biology – it's chemistry! Woman is like man: formed from his very bone and flesh. Yet she is also different: Woman, rather than Man. Once again, women and men are inherently different but inherently similar. This difference within likeness is the basis for their sexual relationship in a lifelong union: 'Therefore . . . they shall become one flesh' (v. 24). Procreation is not mentioned. The emphasis is rather on intimacy and companionship. Sexual difference is about more than fertility: there is something beautiful and significant in the encounter between woman and man.[14]

Deep intimacy and companionship can, of course, exist between people of the same sex – as Jesus himself shows. But whilst procreation is not essential to the 'one flesh' union of marriage, sexual difference is.[15] Once again,

---

[14]*Creation and Covenant*, p. 95.

[15]Not everyone understands 'one flesh' as a reference to sex, e.g. James V. Brownson, *Bible, Gender, Sexuality: Reframing the Church's Debate on Same-Sex Relationships*, (Grand Rapids, MI: Eerdmans, 2013), chapter 5. However, this is how Paul reads it in 1 Corinthians 6:16, as Brownson admits.

anyone who wishes to argue that sex must be within a life-long monogamous relationship but does not need to be between a woman and a man, needs to show why some features of the passage still apply today but not others.

Let's sum things up so far. Whilst there are two creation stories in Genesis 1 and 2, both stress sexual difference. God intended marriage to mean something, and sex within marriage has a particular and beautiful purpose. Sex isn't just a way to make babies, but a gift that brings husband and wife together into physical 'one flesh' union. This physical intimacy expresses and strengthens the bringing together of their lives. Sex has two purposes: procreation (emphasised by Gen. 1), and delight and intimacy between wife and husband (emphasised by Gen. 2). In both cases, the difference between men and women is essential, not accidental. This is why, whatever the excellent virtues of many same-sex relationships, and whatever the rights of providing them with legal protection and support, they cannot be regarded as marriage. Biblically speaking, sexual differentiation is inherent to marriage. And, if these relationships are good but not marriage, they cannot be the right place for sex. As we have seen, sex is an inherent part of marriage, and the Bible consistently regards sex as wrong when it takes place anywhere else.

Does the Bible ever prohibit same-sex activity directly?

As we've seen, there are good and particular theological reasons why sex is for marriage and why the nature of marriage is a lifelong union of one woman and one man. Having looked at these reasons, it is much easier to make sense of the texts which speak directly about same-sex activity. We can now read them within a coherent overall story that explains the rationale behind them.

First, a word about two biblical episodes that are *not* relevant. They are the very similar stories found in Genesis 19 and Judges 19. Both describe the men of a city (Sodom and Gibeah respectively) attempting to 'know' (i.e. have sex with) men who are staying the night as guests of an inhabitant of the city. In both cases, the host offers a woman or women to the crowd instead, and in Judges 19 the woman is abused so badly that she dies.

The reason that these two stories do not reflect on same-sex activity as such is that both cases involve attempted rape. Rape is wrong regardless of the sex of the victim in relation to their attacker, and the actions of the men of Sodom and Gibeah are just as repulsive to gay people as to anyone else. So whilst it is true that these passages clearly disapprove of the men of Sodom and Gibeah, it is misleading to suggest that this disapproval is relevant for thinking about loving and consensual same-sex intimacy.

Other verses, however, do comment on same-sex activity in much more general terms. Perhaps the most well known is Leviticus 18:22, 'You shall not lie with a male as with a woman; it is an abomination.'[16] This is a blanket prohibition of same-sex activity in general terms. However, a genuine question arises about whether this prohibition

---

[16]See also Leviticus 20:13.

should be taken to apply in all times and circumstances. The fact that something is in the Old Testament Law doesn't automatically mean it applies to us today. Few Christians today seek to live out every command in Leviticus literally. The use of this verse to rule out same-sex activity today has therefore been widely ridiculed.

Some of the Old Testament laws are what we might call moral commands, others govern the civil life of the people of Israel in their particular historical circumstances, and still others regulate their religious practices – circumcision, sacrifice, food laws and so on. The moral laws will always be binding (such as the commands not to murder and commit adultery). The historically conditioned civil laws are not literally binding on us, although we can learn from them (priests no longer inspect houses infected with mildew, but health and safety still matter). And, in the case of the religious laws, the New Testament often explicitly gives us reasons why we should no longer obey them. They are fulfilled in Christ and his 'once for all' sacrifice on the cross.

The debate arises, of course, because the Law does not come neatly colour-coded according to these categories. Some things in the wider passage of Leviticus 18 suggest that the prohibition on same-sex activity might be a temporary and religious rule. Many women and men might prefer not to have sex during the woman's period (v. 19), but few would consider it an absolute moral obligation. But apart from verse 19, all the other commands *do* seem to be permanent and moral, ruling out incest, adultery, child sacrifice and bestiality. So, whilst we cannot yet be

100 per cent sure that Leviticus 18:22 is a moral command that applies for all time, it is a strong possibility.

Whenever there is uncertainty about whether an Old Testament command still applies, it is worth asking what the New Testament says on the issue. I think that the New Testament makes it clear that the prohibition on same-sex activity is a permanent and binding one. Two passages are relevant.

The first is 1 Corinthians 6:9–10, in which Paul lists several types of people whom he says will not 'inherit the Kingdom of God', including the sexually immoral, idolaters, thieves, and the greedy. He cannot mean that if you have ever done any of these things, you have blown your chances forever, because he immediately adds, 'And such were some of you. But you were washed, you were sanctified, you were justified in the name of the Lord Jesus Christ and by the Spirit of our God' (v. 11). These sins are serious – but they do not get the last word.

Within the list, Paul uses two Greek words whose meanings have been heavily debated, *malakoi*, and *arsenokoitai* (which also occurs in 1 Tim. 1:9). *Malakoi* literally means 'soft ones.' This was pretty standard language for men who were the 'passive' partner in same-sex intercourse. *Arsenokoitai* is a combination of two other words: *arsen*, meaning 'man', and *koitos*, which means 'bed', but in a particularly sexual sense (it's where we get the word 'coitus' from). So, it's likely to be a reference to male same-sex intercourse, especially given its proximity to *malakoi*. Significantly, *arsen* and *koitos* both occur together in the Greek translation of the Old Testament, the Septuagint.

There, they are used to translate – guess what – Leviticus 18:22. So it seems pretty clear that Paul is here picking up the Old Testament prohibition of same-sex activity, and by using both *malakoi* and *arsenokoitai*, he is referring to both partners in male same-sex intercourse.

The second New Testament passage is Romans 1:26–28, which is the only place where same-sex desire (not just activity), and female homosexuality are mentioned. Paul wrote these verses in the middle of a long description of sin and its effects on humanity. The heart of sin is that humans (as a whole) 'suppress the truth' (v. 18) by wilfully ignoring the evident reality of God in creation (v. 20) and substituting idols for God. It is in this context that Paul says that 'women exchanged natural relations for those that are contrary to nature; and the men likewise gave up natural relations with women and were consumed with passion for one another' (vv. 26–27). Paul is not singling out these individuals for special criticism. Rather, he is saying that the existence of these desires is one of the consequences (not the only one – he mentions plenty of others) of humanity's general turning away from nature in order to ignore God. For Paul, it is so obviously 'contrary to nature' (v. 26) that it is for him an example of how far humanity has gone from the way God originally made us.

The words translated 'contrary to nature' (*para phusin* in Greek) have generated great debate. One argument is that 'nature' is not a reference to human nature as such, but the nature of that particular person, i.e. it refers to straight men who give up their straight nature to have sex with other men. Because we now (supposedly) know that there is a fixed, permanent gay orientation, this does not apply. Others suggest that the dominant types of same-sex activity at the time were prostitution and pederasty, and so these texts should not be taken to refer to permanent, consenting adult relationships.

I find these arguments highly unconvincing. They rely on reading Paul in the light of a particular modern interpretation of sexuality. And the fact is that there *were* adult, consenting same-sex relationships in the ancient world.[17] Paul's comments here don't suggest that same-sex activity is problematic because it is exploitative or abusive, but precisely because it involves two people of the same sex exchanging or giving up 'natural relations' with people of the opposite sex (vv. 26–27).

In conclusion, we have seen that the Old Testament contains a blanket prohibition of (male) same-sex activity. On its own, we can't tell for sure whether this was intended as a temporary legal or ceremonial command, or whether it expresses a permanent moral norm. But in the New Testament, at least two texts suggest that the prohibition is a permanent one. 1 Corinthians 6:9–10 uses the same language as the Greek version of Leviticus 18:22, and Romans 1 describes same-sex desire and activity (including between women) as 'contrary to nature'.

Plus, all this needs to be set in the context of the general biblical view (especially found in Genesis and in the

---

[17]See the article by Peter Ould in footnote 4 above, and Thomas K. Hubbard (ed.), *Homosexuality in Greece and Rome: A Sourcebook of Basic Documents* (Los Angeles, CA: University of California Press, 2003).

teaching of Jesus) that sex is a good gift for marriage, and that marriage is between a woman and a man. Given the strong emphasis in the Bible on female-male complementarity as an essential feature of marriage, the explicit prohibition of same-sex activity is exactly what we would expect to find. This complementarity is part of marriage for important and specific theological reasons.

It is not that the Bible singles out same-sex activity for more attention than any other sexual sin. It also rules out adultery, promiscuity, pre-marital sex, and so on. But these and same-sex activity are all ruled out for the same reason, namely that they involve sex taking place in a context other than the one it was made for: marriage between a woman and a man.

If two people love each other, why shouldn't they express that love through sex?

When the Gestapo arrested Dietrich Bonhoeffer, he was working on a book called *Ethics*. In it, he points out that Paul in 1 Corinthians 13 says that one can possess all manner of worthy characteristics (such as prophetic powers), do good deeds (give one's possessions to the poor), even undergo martyrdom – yet be without love.[18] This should make us pause before being too confident that we all know what love means.

Similarly, Bonhoeffer says, the verse 'God is love' (1 John 4:16) is persistently misread because we think that

---

[18]Dietrich Bonhoeffer, *Ethics*, tr. Ilse Tödt et al., ed. Eberhard Bethge et al. (Minneapolis, MN: Fortress, 2009), p. 332.

we understand the word 'love', and use that in order to understand God. Bonhoeffer thinks it should be the other way around: in order to understand love, we first need to know God.[19] God's love exists before our love and is the basis of our love: 'In this is love, not that we have loved God but that he loved us' (1 John 4:10). And the form that this takes is the cross of Christ: 'This is how we know what love is: Jesus Christ laid down his life for us' (1 John 3:16, NIV).

The argument that 'surely what matters is that two people love each other' is based on the human-centred understanding of love which Bonhoeffer criticises.[20] We should not infer the nature of love from people's experiences and feelings, if this means setting aside the theological significance of the difference between men and women as set out above. In other words, we need to understand love through Christian revelation, not through the human experience of love.

The reason for this is that human love, just like human everything else, is fallen. We cannot simply read off how we should act from how we feel. Our ability to observe

---

[19] *Ethics*, p. 334.

[20] Here is one example: 'Suppose two people loved each other with all their hearts, and they wanted to commit themselves to each other in the sight of God . . . to serve God together; to be faithful for the rest of their lives. If they were people of opposite sexes, we would call that holy and beautiful . . . But if we changed only one thing – the gender of one of those individuals – while still keeping the same love and selflessness and commitment, suddenly many Christians would call it abominable.' Justin Lee, *Unconditional: Rescuing the Gospel from the Gays-vs-Christians Debate* (London: Hodder & Stoughton, 2013), p. 185.

and think about ourselves is not fully reliable and our lives are fraught with self-deception. Plus we are no longer the way God originally intended us to be, in many respects. But the gospel and Jesus's teaching are clear.

Hence, even our love needs to be remade in the light of the cross and of Jesus's teaching. We must bring even our noblest and deepest feelings to Christ for him to revolutionise and transform them. As Paul puts it, love 'rejoices with the truth' (1 Cor. 13:6). We cannot know if love is love on its own. It needs the truth.

In my own case, it was precisely experiencing God's love that meant I did not simply go along with the pattern of my sexual feelings. It was God's love which led me to rejoice in the truth of my creation as a physically sexual being, which is what orders me towards either marriage or celibacy. The desire for a committed, sexually intimate relationship and the desire for intimacy with people of the same sex are not wrong desires. These desires are originally good and beautiful aspects of the way God has made us all. But for me, part of being fallen is that these two originally separate but good desires have been muddled up together. Therefore, I can't define love by my own perceptions or by how I feel. I have to look at who God says that I am. By not starting with my own experience of love, but letting myself be loved by God, I eventually came to an outcome that was not what I had expected at all, namely marriage.

Conclusion

I've tried to show here not only that Scripture rules out same-sex activity, which I think it does, but why.

We saw that Jesus's own view of sexual morality was founded on the creation stories in Genesis 1 and 2. By looking at those stories, we discovered that the classic Christian teaching on sex and marriage isn't a minor or peripheral theme within the biblical story. It is integral to central aspects of Christian faith, including Jesus's teaching about the nature of marriage, the Triune reality of God, the doctrine of union with Christ, the relationship between Christ and the church, and the goodness of human bodily existence. This is why when Scripture explicitly mentions same-sex activity, it does so in a 'consistently negative' way.[21]

Picture a woolly jumper with a loose thread sticking out. It looks messy and it spoils the whole jumper. So it's very tempting to yank the thread out. But when you pull it, instead of snapping, a bit more thread comes out with it. You could keep pulling, and pulling. More and more thread would keep coming out until the whole jumper was ruined because, at the end of the day, the jumper as a whole *is* thread.

The classic view of sexual morality is a bit like that. It seems inconvenient today. It's certainly unpopular. Some claim that it's putting gay people and others off church (although I actually doubt this claim). So, what could be simpler than to yank out and get rid of this unsightly and seemingly peripheral teaching? The problem is, as I hope I have shown, that this teaching is connected to many

---

[21]Christopher R. Seitz, *The Character of Christian Scripture* (Grand Rapids, MI: Baker Academic, 2011), pp. 176,178.

other things. If we yank out this teaching by saying that sometimes sex is OK outside marriage after all, we will have to find an alternative way of explaining why we still think that adultery and promiscuity are wrong. If we yank it out by expanding our definition of marriage beyond Jesus's definition of it as the one-flesh union of a woman and a man, then marriage will no longer be the wonderful picture of the gospel that it was intended to be. If sexual difference is not relevant for sexual union, even our account of God as Trinity, real difference within perfect union, is affected. If we keep pulling the thread, we may be shocked at how long it is, and how much of the jumper ends up coming out with it.

Go Deeper

For a very full discussion of the Bible and recent interpretations of it, see Martin Davie, *Studies on the Bible and Same-Sex Relationships since 2003* (Malton, N. Yorks: Gilead Books, 2015). A shorter Summary version is also available.

Lisa Diamond, 'Just How Different are Female and Male Sexual Orientation?' a lecture, online at http://www.cornell.edu/video/lisa-diamond-on-sexual-fluidity-of-men-and-women.

Christopher C. Roberts, *Creation and Covenant: The Significance of Sexual Difference in the Moral Theology of Marriage* (London: T & T Clark, 2007).

Jenell Williams Paris, *The End of Sexual Identity: Why Sex is Too Important to Define Who We Are* (Downers Grove, IL: IVP, 2011).

Why have so many Christians modernised their attitude to slavery and divorce, but not to homosexuality? Does this show that the church is homophobic?

- On slavery, see my article here: http://www.livingout.org/if-we-ve-rejected-what-the-bible-says-about-slavery-why-not-reject-what-it-says-about-homosexuality-too-.
- On divorce, see the companion study on divorce in my The *Only Way is Ethics* series.

Sexual Singleness

Why singleness is good, and practical thoughts on being single and sexual

Singleness is not an academic issue for me. Soon after I became a Christian, I realised that I was gay. I was part of a wonderful youth congregation that did not shy away from teaching about real life issues, and pretty quickly I got the message that it was OK to be gay, but that I shouldn't act on my sexual orientation: sex is a good gift, but only to be used in marriage between a man and a woman. So I assumed that I would remain single for life.

Here, I'll unpack some theology that explains why singleness is hard, but also why it can be deeply fulfilling and needs to be valued much more highly by the church. In fact, I'm going to argue that singleness is *better* than marriage – not a standard view in church! I'll look at the question of whether Jesus was single, and show how we all need intimate friendship in order to be fulfilled. Then I'll take this theology and apply it to some really practical questions, such as whether Christians should marry non-Christians, how you can be sexual without having sex, masturbation, living a fulfilled life whatever your situation, and how the church can value and support single people better. Let's kick off by looking at why singleness is so hard in the first place.

Why is singleness as a Christian so hard today?

Many people think it's preposterous, even dangerous to go without sex. They believe that sex is just a consensual arrangement between two adults for mutual enjoyment – and an inherent part of being fulfilled. This view puts pressure on single Christians who seek to live within the classic Christian belief that sex is a gift for marriage. Movies such as *The 40-Year-Old Virgin* mock the idea of someone reaching the age of 40 without ever having this supposedly essential human experience.[1]

And in church, many single Christians feel abnormal for not being married. Leadership may be based around couples, and churches may emphasise 'family' ministry, even holding 'family services' (also painful for couples dealing with infertility). Some churches run marriage courses, provide marriage preparation, and publicly congratulate people when they get engaged – but where is the equivalent investment in and celebration of living well as a single person? Even (urgently needed) teaching on godly dating and relationships can make it seem as if the goal is to escape singleness by getting married.

The message from the church seems to be that marriage is the norm and singleness is a temporary state on the way. Many people therefore feel marginalised, as if they are a spare 'half' waiting around for someone else to complete them. This is an unrealistic prospect for many Christian women, because the church has far more single women members than men.

Of course, many people are single because they are divorced or their spouse has died. And some Christians remain single because of their sexuality – they are not attracted to anyone of the opposite sex and are committed to remaining celibate.

---

[1] *The 40-Year-Old Virgin*, dir. Judd Apatow, (Universal Pictures, 2005).

So, single Christians are caught between a rock and a hard place: trying to be sexually pure in a sex-obsessed world, and trying to be fulfilled in a church that seems obsessed with marriage.[2] We have to do better than this!

Is singleness meant to be this hard?

The pressure many single people in the church feel to marry (and the sense of failure and incompleteness they may feel if they don't) is unfair and unnecessary. Embracing a more biblical theology of sex and singleness would alleviate this. But whilst we need to become more positive about singleness, we must not deny how hard it can be. I recently visited a church to preach about homosexuality, and in doing so spoke positively about singleness, wanting to affirm and honour those who are living this way. But a woman said afterwards that I had caused her pain. In my rush to affirm the goodness of singleness, I had skated over its challenge and cost.

The Bible gives a reason for this heartache. Although everything that God makes is 'very good' (Gen. 1:31), Genesis 2 identifies a seeming lack in what God has made: 'It is not good that the man should be alone' (v. 18). Humanity is not designed for solitude, but for relationship and community. Thus, here is the element of truth in the idea that marriage is the norm or ideal: at this stage in God's unfolding plan for the world, marriage (and procreation) gives the primary solution to the problem of human solitude. This is

---

[2]For more on this theme, I recommend the brilliant book by my friend Kate Wharton, *Single Minded: Being Single, Whole and Living Life to the Full* (Oxford: Monarch, 2013), ch. 2 – 4.

why the majority of single people would prefer to be married, having one particular person with whom to share their lives. We should dwell on this point for two reasons.

First, we see that even though the Bible teaches that singleness is very good, it is costly. Not only because single people experience pressure from the church and the world, but also because God made us for an intimate relationship with another person. He made our bodies for sex and our hearts for love. So, singleness can be wonderful, and used by God, but it can involve loneliness and unfulfilled sexual desire and hopes, such as to have children.[3] Of course, marriage is also very challenging. Most married people experience loneliness at times, and some chronically. Some married couples have unfulfilled hopes for children as well. But no matter how much single people have good friends and community around them, they still face the particular cost of singleness in terms of sexual abstinence and not having one particular person who is committed to them for life.

The second point about Genesis 2:18 is more surprising: *God is not enough for us.* God does not say, 'it is not good that the man should be alone; I had better stick around,' but, 'I will make him a companion.'[4] Some

---

[3]See 'Sex and the Single Woman' by Fabienne Harford, online at http://www.thegospelcoalition.org/article/sex-and-the-single-woman.

[4]My translation. Although the Hebrew word *ezer* can be translated 'helper', this sounds as though Eve's role is to serve Adam. But *ezer* usually refers to God as the 'helper' of Israel, so it certainly does not imply subordination.

Christians believe that they must find fulfilment in God alone, an idea that has crept into the lyrics of quite a few worship songs. So, when I was single, I thought that the solution to loneliness was to keep growing in my intimacy and relationship with God. That helped, of course. But as I drew closer to God, I discovered something I didn't expect: God was not enough! I needed to be close to other humans too, because God made us to need and care for one another. This is part of what makes us truly human.

Was Jesus single?

So, the Bible explains why singleness is hard. But keep turning the pages of the Bible and you'll discover that is not the whole story. Marriage is good, but it is not the only route to fulfilment. The most powerful reason to believe this, is the life and example of Jesus.

Jesus probably never married.[5] If he did, why did the writers of all four gospels think it was so unimportant that they never bothered to mention it? They tell us about his parents, his relatives (Elizabeth, Zechariah and John the Baptist), the way Mary and Joseph discovered Mary's pregnancy, Jesus's birth, and the fact that he had brothers and sisters (Mark 6:3 even gives his brothers' names). The early church was a family affair – Jesus's mother Mary, and one or two of his brothers (James and perhaps Jude) were prominent within it.

Singleness was very unusual for a rabbi of Jesus's day. So if he had been married, the church would not have

---

[5] I am grateful to Dr Ian Paul, who helped me develop these arguments.

needed to cover it up. And, as we shall see, Jesus being single fits well with his own teaching about marriage, which was very radical. So, whilst we can't totally prove that Jesus was single, it seems very likely that the gospels would have mentioned his wife and children if he'd had any.

Singleness and fulfilment

So Jesus was probably unmarried. Paul was *definitely* unmarried (at least when he wrote 1 Corinthians), and he intended to stay that way. So the New Testament is dominated by single people! But in the Jewish and Roman context of Jesus and Paul, singleness was much more unusual than today. Marriage was compulsory under Roman law (otherwise Roman men just enjoyed casual affairs and never got round to having legitimate heirs). Having children was a public duty! Marriage was not compulsory in Judaism, but singleness was very unusual because the Old Testament valued marriage and procreation so highly.

Yet it seems obvious that Jesus was more fulfilled than you and me. If not, why follow him? Indeed, he lived the most fulfilled life possible. So, being human and fulfilled does not have to include marriage and sex. Jesus lived the most fulfilled life that has ever been lived without either.

And, as we will see, Jesus taught that in the new creation, even though we will still be physical, bodily creatures, and we will still be men and women, marriage and sex will not exist. Yet we will be perfectly fulfilled without them. We won't miss sex!

This is a development from the Old Testament. There, we saw that marriage is God's primary answer to human solitude. But in the New Testament, sex and marriage are not necessary for fulfilment. Sure, sex is nice. And singleness can be hard. But Jesus shows us that you can live a deeply fulfilled life (I didn't say an easy life) without sex and marriage.

Friendship and intimacy

Jesus shows us that we can be fulfilled without sex. But we can't be fulfilled without *intimacy*. Jesus might not have been married, but he needed family and friends. God becoming human meant being born into a normal family. Jesus was vulnerable and dependent on others for his physical and emotional needs.

This is equally true in Jesus's adult life. Although he ministered to multitudes and had many encounters with individuals, Jesus deliberately ordered his life around a small group of people – not servants, but friends (John 15:13–15). They ate together and shared their money. Even when Jesus sent his friends out on mission, he sent them in pairs, not alone (Mark 6:7).

Amongst his twelve closest followers, Jesus had a particular inner circle of three (Peter, James and John). This privileged relationship was partly a matter of teaching and training them, but they were also the ones he wanted with him for company and prayerful support in his agonising distress in Gethsemane (Matt. 26:37).

One friend was so close to Jesus that this friend describes himself as 'the disciple whom Jesus loved' (e.g. John 20:2). Jesus confides the identity of his betrayer to the beloved disciple (John 13:23 – note that Peter, the leader, knows that the best way to get this information from Jesus is to ask this disciple). And when Jesus is dying, it's the beloved disciple he asks to look after his mother (John 19:26–27). We find the 'beloved' description confusing, because Jesus loves everyone! But Jesus still needed friends to help him and to share with, just like the rest of us.

Some people today speculate that this deep same-sex friendship must have been a homoerotic or sexual one. This says more about our obsession with sex than about the reality of the friendship. Indeed, many in the ancient world believed that friendship between two men could be far closer than between a married couple, so we're mistaken to read sexual undertones into the fact that Jesus 'loved' this disciple.

This matters, because our tendency to see intimacy in sexual terms makes it harder for us to form deep friendships. We fear that our feelings will become sexual, or that our friendship will be misinterpreted. Because of my sexuality, I used to hold back from deep friendships with other guys, partly because I was scared I might develop feelings for them. (I now tease my male friends that I solve this by only having ugly friends.) Similarly, I believe that straight people of the opposite sex can have close friendships – just as Jesus formed friendships with women as well as men (Mary and Martha in John 11:5 and Luke 10:38–42). Of course, if you really have the hots for someone, it would be dumb to seek a deep friendship with them. And sometimes two friends develop an inappropriate attraction. But that can be dealt with through honesty, sensible boundaries and good accountability. We can't let the mere possibility hold us back from deep friendships.

Our tendency to see intimate relationships in sexual terms can even hinder friendship between straight people of the same sex. I know a single woman who had a close female friend who was teased by other Christians for having a so-called girlfriend. Yet here were two people seeking to live godly and fulfilling lives. Their friendship helped them do this. They should have been applauded as a good example, rather than treated with suspicion. This will only put people off friendship. Married or single, we *all* need friendship. But intentionally cultivating this life-sharing friendship is particularly essential for single people, and we'll look at this more below.

The Church is our true and eternal family

Jesus lived a fulfilled life in friendship and community. He did not dismiss marriage and family life, but the community he formed around himself was much more important: the church. Shockingly, for a Jew of his day, when members of his human family were waiting outside to see him, he did this: 'Looking about at those who sat around him, he said, "Here are my mother and my brothers! For whoever does the will of God, he is my brother and sister and mother"' (Mark 3:34–35). He ignores his family, and says that they are not really his family! Our human family may be good, bad or ugly (or usually a mix of all three), but the church is now our true family and our primary human community.

Jesus also taught that marriage is fundamentally temporary. Some Sadducees (who did not believe in the resurrection) presented a scenario to Jesus in which a woman married seven men. They asked, 'In the resurrection, therefore, of the seven, whose wife will she be?' (Matt.22:28). Jesus retorted, 'In the resurrection they neither marry nor are given in marriage, but are like angels in heaven' (v. 30). Marriage is good, but temporary.

This is because part of the purpose of marriage is to reflect the relationship between Christ and the church (e.g. Eph. 5:31–32). When Jesus returns, the union between Jesus and his people will be perfected, so we won't need marriage to point to it. So, marriage is temporary, but the church is eternal.

This perspective made the early church very radical. People who were seen as inferior by wider society, such as women, slaves and the poor, were meant to be treated equally to rich free men. Fellow Christians were 'brothers and sisters'. Churches usually met in houses, and Peter and Paul describe the church as an *oikos* – a household or family. This even means that Christians should show one another physical affection, and several times Paul instructs people to 'greet one another with a holy kiss' (e.g. Rom. 16:16). This seems normal to us – but it was very strange in his day to encourage physical touch between people who were not related to one another. But they *were* related, through Christ.

This challenges us all. Married people: do you get your sense of identity and security from the fact that you are married? When I'm having a bad day, it is easy to expect my wife to cheer me up, or to think, 'At least my kids love me!' And it is good and natural to receive love and support this way. But it is easy to idolise these good things if they eclipse my primary identity as a child of God and part of Jesus's body. It is easy to hold back from serving in church because of my family commitments, or never to make time for other friends. Plus, it puts unfair pressure on my family to meet all my needs.

And if you are single, it is not wrong to want to be married. But keep it in perspective. It's tempting to yearn for marriage so much that you forget you are *already* part of the most important and fulfilling human community. Marriage does not solve anyone's problems or make life easier, nor can it bring ultimate fulfilment. Just as I can treat my family as an idol, so the search for a partner can become a distraction from our primary community, the church. It is not wrong to want one special person with whom to share your life. But one person is not enough. Even God always has two! That's why we need church.

Marriage is good - but singleness is better

The New Testament goes even further than this. Marriage is still seen as good – it reflects the way God originally made us. But singleness is better, because it anticipates the new creation. It foreshadows and lives out a little bit of eternity here and now. (Saying singleness is better is not the same as saying that singleness is easy!)

Paul teaches directly that singleness is better than marriage. In 1 Corinthians 7 he begins, 'It is good for a man not to have sexual relations with a woman' (v. 1). He may be quoting from a letter *from* the Corinthians. Some of them believed that being spiritual meant avoiding supposedly nasty physical things like sex. (Others went to the opposite extreme of believing they could do what they liked with their bodies and it wouldn't affect them spiritually.) So, Paul reminds married couples not to give up sex, except temporarily and by mutual agreement (v. 5).

So, Paul is not against marriage and sex. But note why he thinks someone should marry: 'If they cannot exercise self-control, they should marry. For it is better to marry than to burn with passion' (v. 9). This is hardly a ringing endorsement! Paul is not encouraging marriage for its own sake so much as saying that marriage is better than sexual sin (see v. 2: 'because of the temptation to sexual immorality, each man should have his own wife and each woman her own husband').

But Paul's real preference is singleness: 'I wish that all were as I myself am' (v. 7). Nobody is obliged to be single, but it is better. Of course, if you are already married, you must stay that way: everyone should 'remain in the condition' in which they were when they became Christians (v. 20). So single people should seek to remain single, unless they cannot control themselves sexually (although this category includes nearly everyone at one time or another).

What about people who are betrothed? Again, it is better for them not to marry, because of the imminent return of Jesus: 'for the present form of this world is passing away' (v. 31). The new creation is on its way, when there will be no marriage. Jesus's return has only grown nearer since then.

Paul then explains why singleness is better than marriage: single people are less burdened by worldly anxieties and can focus on serving God more wholeheartedly. 'The married man is anxious about worldly things, how to please his wife, and his interests are divided. And the unmarried or betrothed woman is anxious about the things of the Lord, how to be holy in body and spirit' (vv. 33–34). Marriage is good, but a potential distraction. So singleness is better, if you can keep your sexual desires under control. It enables an 'undivided devotion to the Lord' (v. 35) – which we see in the many single people who have made a remarkable impact for God in mission, prayer, theology and so on.

As theologian and musician Kathryn Wehr points out, in the early church some thought that this was why Jesus said resurrected humanity would be 'like angels'. Angels are completely tuned in to God and surrendered to his will. They are able to do what he wants right away.[6] Paul concludes, 'So then he who marries his betrothed does well, and he who refrains from marriage will do even better' (v. 38). Marriage is good – but singleness is better.

As promised, it's now time to take the theology we've looked at and see how it applies to the big practical questions of singleness. And one of the most challenging is whether Christians should only marry one another. Let's start with that.

Should Christians only marry other Christians?

In 1 Corinthians 7:39 we find the clearest statement in the New Testament that Christians should only marry other

_____
[6]Kathryn Wehr, *Singleness and the Early Church: Encouragement for Living the Single Life in Christ Today* (Cambridge: Grove, 2012), pp. 7–8.

Christians: 'A wife is bound to her husband as long as he lives. But if her husband dies, she is free to be married to whom she wishes, only in the Lord.'

First, the good news. As we've seen, the New Testament introduces significant freedom to the question of whether you should get married. Each person, under God, must discern their own calling. Similarly, here Paul emphasises our freedom over whom to marry: 'to whom she wishes'. I am not saying that arranged marriages are completely prohibited. But even when an arranged marriage has been proposed, the couple themselves must still make up their own minds.

Now the challenging news: Paul does specify that a believer with this free choice should only marry another believer, 'in the Lord', although if a Christian does get married to a non-Christian, Paul is clear that such marriages are completely valid marriages (vv. 12–16).

My wife and I are both Christians. And our marriage takes hard work: on communication, making sacrifices, facing tricky decisions, forgiving each other, and so on. And that is with a committed fellow Christian. Of course many non-Christians are very supportive of their spouse's faith, nevertheless living life with someone who does not ultimately share your values and understand you at your deepest level definitely adds a layer of complexity for most people.

Of course, this advice may seem fatuous to many single Christians, especially women, because they do not have the luxury of choosing between singleness and marriage to a Christian. They may feel, as Paul says elsewhere, that 'it is better to marry than to burn with passion' (1 Cor. 7:9). This brings us to the crucial question of what to do with unfulfilled sexual desire, as a single person.

Being single and sexual

There is no point pretending that living without sex is easy. For most single people, sexual abstinence sometimes or often leads to physical and emotional frustration which can be very intense. Some friends and I run a website called 'Living Out', the subject of which is ostensibly homosexuality. But the most frequently viewed page, written by my friend Ed Shaw, is entitled, 'How can you live life without sex?'[7] Plenty of straight people are asking that question too.

It may help to remember that being a sexual person is not just about whether you have sex or not. People who believe that sex is for marriage can end up running away from or scared of the fact that they are *already* sexual beings as women and men. Sexuality is about a lot more than our genitalia: it affects the way we dress and present ourselves to others, the way we interact with other people, our sense of identity.

For example, every so often my wife goes out with 'the girls'. She has a bath, chooses nice clothes and puts on jewellery and make-up. These things help her look and feel good about herself and her body. They express and celebrate her sexuality, but they have nothing to do with having sex.

---

[7] Ed Shaw, 'How can you live life without sex?' online at http://www.livingout.org/how-can-you-live-life-without-sex-.

Jesus himself was a sexual being. In becoming fully human, by definition he had to become either male or female. Being sexual is not sinful – and you are sexual whether you actually have sex or not. Recognising this provides a healthy basis for sexual self-acceptance. Your sexuality mustn't be repressed, but *integrated* with your faith. I share how this worked out in my own life in *Living Out My Story*. See also 'Go Deeper' at the end of this discussion for resources with more practical guidance on this.

Masturbation

Masturbation causes a huge amount of guilt and shame for many people (married and single). Is masturbation a legitimate, healthy release of sexual desire when it has nowhere else to go, or a sinful and selfish transgression of sexual boundaries?

See the next page for what the Bible has to say about masturbation:

[This page intentionally left blank]

That is, the Bible never says that masturbation is a sin. Some have fancifully read this into the episode of Onan spilling his semen on the ground (Gen. 38:9), but Onan's sin was trying to prevent his brother from having an heir by using the withdrawal method of contraception. The Law refers rather quaintly to men having 'nocturnal emissions' (Deut. 23:10). This could refer to spontaneous ejaculation (wet dreams), or it could be a reference to masturbation. If so, it's significant that the Law doesn't treat it as a sin, but as a ceremonial impurity.

Of course, silence on an issue in the Bible does not automatically mean it is OK. If it is a form of sex outside marriage, then it is an abuse of the gift of sex. It is taking sexual pleasure for oneself without any of the commitment to and care for another person that sex within marriage involves. But if masturbation is such a heinous sin, I still find it surprising that the Bible never troubles to say so.

But God is unambiguously opposed to lust. Jesus said: 'Everyone who looks at a woman with lustful intent has already committed adultery with her in his heart' (Matt. 5:28). Lust demeans a precious person who has been created in God's image. It treats them as an object for your own gratification. And, in a day when pornography is available at the click of a button, lust is clearly a huge temptation. Perhaps masturbation without lust is possible purely as a physical release of sexual tension. But lust and masturbation are usually very closely connected. Rather than relieving lustful desire, it can also stimulate it. So, whilst I am reluctant to say outright that masturbation is a sin, it could be playing with fire, and hinder the pursuit of a healthy, integrated sexuality.

From theology to reality: some practical suggestions

I want to conclude by suggesting some ways in which the theology I have outlined can make a positive, practical difference. I write this with trepidation, aware that it has been quite a while since I was single (although, as I share in *Living Out My Story*, I thought I would be single for life).

1. Live life to the full, whatever your situation

Try asking yourself this question. If God/an angel/the Bible[8] suddenly told you that you were going to remain single for the rest of your life, how would it affect your life? Would you live your life differently? Are there dreams or callings that you have been putting on hold until you knew whether or not you would get married?

Maybe you wouldn't do anything differently. Or maybe you would get on with certain things, make different choices about where you live, what you do, church involvement, family life and friendships. Don't miss out on anything that God has for you because you are waiting to get married first. See marriage as a bonus, not as a prerequisite for living fully. If you don't get married, that could still be painful, but at least you won't be missing out on living life to the full. Don't keep a 'hope chest' under your bed, literally or metaphorically – just get it out and start enjoying life.

I have friends who felt called to adopt children when they were single. They wanted to get married but they

---

[8]Select according to your theological preference.

refused to wait around, in case it didn't ever happen. Of course, not everyone is called to parent on their own. But the principle is: don't let being single hold you back from fulfilling God's call, whatever that might be for you. Sometimes marriage even makes things harder, not easier.

If having a relationship or getting married is your goal, singleness can only be about coping as best you can, for as short a time as possible. Learning to live a content and full life will benefit any future marriage anyway. But getting married in order to escape from some perceived deficit will not solve any problems – it will just inflict them onto someone else!

2. Healthy and fulfilled singleness doesn't just happen

Many churches run marriage preparation courses, marriage retreats, marriage this, that and the other. We recognise that marriage needs good preparation and ongoing investment. Here's the big secret: *so does singleness.*

A friend once said to me, 'I just wish I knew one way or another whether I would get married or not. If I knew I would stay single, I would be disappointed, but I could grieve and move on. It would be so much easier to plan out my life if I just knew.' When I thought I was going to be single permanently, that forced me to work out what I would need and intentionally seek support from friends and mentors.

Again, if you knew you were going to stay single, how would you prepare and what would you need? Examples might include who you live with, where you live, the kind of work you do, involvement in church and ministry, healthy physical touch, having a mentor or spiritual director, fun and leisure, feeling appreciated and valued, spending time on your own and spending time with others, and so on. It is healthy and right to seek out good ways of meeting these legitimate needs.

3. You can live without sex, but you can't live without intimacy

A few godly and gifted people are able to live a sexually pure life in isolation. But most of us need help! In Christianity, people committed to celibacy usually joined a community of other celibates. This is partly in order to have accountability and support in the battle for purity. But more importantly, it is because we all need people to share our lives with. That is how God made us.

Once when preaching I talked about needing deep friendships. But someone pointed out to me afterwards that depth is not enough. She had deep friendships. What she missed was someone to share shallow things with. Maybe 80 per cent of marriage is the 'shallow' stuff: emptying the dishwasher, sharing how your day went, watching a movie, knowing someone will miss you when you're away. Intimacy is built on small things.

Living well as a single person means sharing life with others on a day-to-day basis. This was exactly what Jesus did. As Mark's gospel puts it, Jesus 'appointed twelve . . . *so that they might be with him* and he might send them out to preach' (3:14, my emphasis). Jesus did not gather disciples just so he could send them to preach. First and foremost they were called to 'be with him', to share life together.

I think this is the single biggest change we need to make in church. Rather than seeing singleness as being on your own and marriage as being together, everyone needs people with whom to share their lives. This might mean single people and/or married couples choosing to live with one another in a community with a loosely agreed way of life. Or it might be as simple as the way you choose your flatmates.

How can the church support single people seeking to live a godly life?[9]

A full, contented single life does not just happen. It takes investment from the individual – but it should matter to the whole church too. Church leaders, in particular, have a responsibility to prepare and equip people to live well. Here are a few suggestions as to how:

1. Think of singleness as a way of life for all. We will all be single at one time, and probably more than once – especially at a time when people marry later in life and when so many marriages break up.
2. Churches should be places of healthy, appropriate physical touch and affection. In one survey, twice as many single people identified lack of touch as being one of the hardest things about being single, rather

[9]This section draws on some of the suggestions made by Kate Wharton in *Single Minded* (Oxford: Monarch, 2013), which I highly recommend.

than lack of sex. Our bodies are a good and beautiful part of how God has made us, and they need to be affirmed and loved through touch, not just words. How can we 'greet one another with a holy kiss' in our churches?

3. Nurture the expectation and possibility that single, and quite possibly married people, might consider living together in intentional communities, sharing their lives with one another in deep and seemingly shallow ways.

4. Teach biblically on the value of singleness, and practically on how to live a fulfilling and godly single life. By all means teach about godly dating and relationships, but teach about singleness in its own right too. Don't speak about singleness as a pre-marital state. Provide space for discussion of how this can be done well in your context (that will help you to hear from people what they need, too).

5. Don't imply that singleness is second best, even if you intend to be comforting. For example, 'It's not too late, you'll meet someone.' Comments like this are projections of your own aspirations for that person and assumptions of what is normal. They assume that the person is waiting for something else to happen, as opposed to enjoying life and serving God right now. Also, these platitudes might offer false hope leading to further disappointment.

6. Don't regularly ask after someone's relationship status. It would be rude if single people asked intimate questions about married couples. If they begin a relationship and they want you to know about it, they are perfectly

capable of telling you (or you'll see it on Facebook). Similarly, don't ask anyone why they don't have a boy/girlfriend or tell them they are a good catch. This is intended as a compliment but can makes things worse. There might be a really good reason why they aren't in a relationship (e.g. they just broke up with someone, they are not attracted to people of the opposite sex).

7. Be cautious about matchmaking – especially if you are introducing people to one another for the sake of it. Same-sex attracted people find this especially wearing. If you genuinely think two people might be suitable for one another, have a polite conversation with each of them first. They might not be interested in that person. Or they might not be looking for a relationship at the moment. Or they might be delighted. Take the trouble to find out what *they* think.

8. Don't assume that single people have lots more free time to serve in church or less stressful lives than married people.

9. Teach about good friendships and not just about sex and romantic relationships. When Gaby and I moved to London, we didn't know many people at first. At one point, she told me that she was feeling lonely. My pride was nettled. I protested, 'But I'm with you all the time! Aren't I enough for you?' Quite rightly, her answer was 'No!' She didn't just need a husband – she needed friends too.

10. Ensure that staff and leadership teams contain married and single people, and never assume that leaders need to be part of a couple.

11. Couples and families need to visit single people at home, and not just expect single people to come to them. It may seem easier for a single person to come to a family's home, but it deprives that person of the chance to welcome people into their own home and to offer hospitality.

12. If you are married, don't do everything as a couple – although it's not about having a token single person to hang around with out of pity either. It's about the heart behind your community and relationships: do you see community as something bigger and broader than your nuclear family? If so, it will be natural to include others, and it won't feel strained.

Conclusion

Singleness, like marriage, can be a hard road to walk. But it is not second best. Singleness, like marriage, needs intentional investment and support, if it is to be the fulfilling way of life that God intended it to be – namely, a beautiful witness to the way that we will all be in the new creation.

Go Deeper

Donald Goergen, *The Sexual Celibate* (Colorado Springs, CO: Image Books, 1979). Older, but still well worth a read.

William F. Kraft, *Whole and Holy Sexuality: How to Find Human and Spiritual Integrity as a Sexual Person* (Eugene, OR: Wipf and Stock, 1989).

Vaughan Roberts, *True Friendship: Walking Shoulder to Shoulder* (Leyland, Lancs: 10Publishing, 2013).

Ed Shaw, 'How can you live life without sex?' online at http://www.livingout.org/how-can-you-live-life-without-sex-.

Kathryn Wehr, *Singleness and the Early Church: Encouragement for Living the Single Life in Christ Today* (Cambridge: Grove Books, 2012).

Kate Wharton, *Single Minded* (Oxford: Monarch, 2013).

As Long as You Love Me

Divorce and Remarriage

Marriage is popular. In England and Wales, there are about a quarter of a million weddings a year. But only a tiny proportion of people are virgins when they marry, and 85 per cent of couples are already living together when they tie the knot. It's estimated that 42 per cent of all marriages in England and Wales end in divorce.[1] Divorce doesn't necessarily put people off – in more than a third of marriages today, one or both partners have been married previously.[2] So the popularity of marriage doesn't necessarily mean that people are signing up to the Christian ideal (and here as in my other writing in this series I'm assuming marriage as being between a woman and a man).

An older way of seeing marriage was as a way of life or institution. You were free not to join it, but if you did join, you didn't get to set the terms. Now, it's more of a contract. The terms you set should be demanding, because the consumer deserves the best. And if those terms are not met, if your service provider does not live up to your legitimate expectations, then they have broken the contract, and you may walk away. Marriage is conditional on a good performance.

[1]See http://www.ons.gov.uk/ons/rel/vsob1/divorces-in-england-and-wales/2011/sty-what-percentage-of-marriages-end-in-divorce.html. Throughout what follows, I use the most recently available data which is for England and Wales in 2012.

[2]See http://www.ons.gov.uk/ons/rel/vsob1/marriages-in-england-and-wales--provisional-/2012/index.html.

A big influence today is romanticism – the idea that we should be in a relationship with the person that is 'right' for us. (Before marriage of course couples should discern carefully whether they are suited.) The problem comes when romanticism breaks up existing relationships – when one spouse decides someone else is really the right one for them. Rather than being true to their spouse and the bond they already have, they must be true to themselves. New and more powerful feelings of love and romance are more decisive than prior commitments.

The reality is that in marriage you quickly discover that Mr or Mrs Right is not perfect, and neither are you! In any case, sharing your life with another person, in addition to the normal pressures and changes of life, changes you both. A marriage that is conditional on somebody stay-ing the same cannot last: only God is wonderful enough to stay eternally interesting without ever changing. Rather, marriage needs to be secure enough that you can change and grow safely. For this to happen, we have to replace the romantic ideal with something more domes-tic and less glamorous but ultimately more glorious and transformative.[3]

In what follows, I'll look at the legal realities of divorce in the UK today, the reasons why in the Bible God is gen-erally so opposed to divorce, and whether there are cir-cumstances in which it is right to seek divorce or to get

---

[3]See Timothy Keller with Kathy Keller, *The Meaning of Marriage: Facing the Complexities of Marriage with the Wisdom of God* (London: Hodder & Stoughton, 2011), ch. 1.

remarried. I will also offer some suggestions and further resources for those who want to support women who experience domestic abuse.

Divorce today

In Britain today you can't just get divorced. You have to prove that the marriage has already irretrievably broken down on one of several grounds.[4] In 2012, 14 per cent of divorces were on the grounds that one party had committed adultery.[5]

The most common reason, which accounts for 48 per cent of divorces, is that one of the parties had persistently demonstrated 'unreasonable behaviour'. This is probably the most popular ground because it is the quickest route to divorce unless adultery has taken place. 'Unreasonable behaviour' could include physical violence, emotional abuse, addiction, financial irresponsibility, not showing interest in one's spouse, and (persistent) refusal to co-operate with household chores.

Provided the divorce is uncontested, in practice the courts grant divorces for more mild reasons. Let's face it,

[4]Divorce is different to annulment, which is the recognition that a marriage was never valid in the first place (for example, if one of the parties was not of sound mind at the time of the wedding). The Roman Catholic Church also grants religious annulments, which have no legal force.
[5]For this and the statistics that follow, see http://www.ons.gov.uk/ons/rel/vsob1/divorces-in-england-and-wales/2012/stb-divorces-2012.html.

it's not hard to find examples of unreasonable behaviour in any marriage. As one divorce solicitor puts it:

> The courts adopt a realistic attitude. They know that if one party to a marriage . . . issue[s] a divorce petition the marriage has irretrievably broken down . . . and it would be futile to pretend otherwise. The courts therefore adopt quite a relaxed attitude.[6]

Some solicitors therefore advise the petitioner to make the allegations serious enough to warrant divorce, but not serious enough for the other spouse to contest them. The grounds for divorce do not normally prejudice financial settlements and custody of any children, removing a possible incentive for someone to dispute the allegations.

With adultery and unreasonable behaviour, one of the parties is at fault: they caused the marriage to break down. Divorce can also be granted when there is 'no fault', if the couple have been separated for two years and if the other party consents (which accounts for 26 per cent of divorces), or for five years even without consent (which accounts for 12 per cent).

So, the vast majority of divorces in the UK today are either 'no fault' divorces or 'unreasonable behaviour' divorces. Of course, we can't tell from the statistics which of the 56,500 divorces granted for 'unreasonable behaviour' involved cases of cruel or abusive behaviour, and which ones involved the courts being 'relaxed'.

---

[6]'Reasons for Divorce: Unreasonable Behaviour', online at http://www.terry.co.uk/unreasonable_behaviour.html.

It's now time to look at why divorce is so problematic from God's perspective, before we consider when the Bible allows it.

Why is God generally so opposed to divorce?

God values marriage very highly and is generally opposed to divorce. For example: 'The wife should not separate from her husband (but if she does, she should remain unmarried or else be reconciled to her husband), and the husband should not divorce his wife' (1 Cor. 7:10–11). Although Jesus and Paul make exceptions to this principle, it is clearly a strong one. To many people today this seems legalistic and unrealistic, so it's important to explore why the Bible is so opposed to divorce and remarriage in general – for theologically important and pastorally loving reasons.

1. Divorce rips apart two people that God has bound together as 'one flesh' (Gen. 2:24). This is the reason that Jesus himself gives as to why divorce should not take place: 'What therefore God has joined together, let not man separate' (Matt. 19:6). He does not say nobody *can* separate, but that nobody *should* do so.[7] Divorce is so painful and devastating because there cannot be a neat separation of two different people: they have become one. This is true whether the marriage is between Christians or not.

---

[7]This is why I find the Roman Catholic view that divorce is impossible unconvincing. For that teaching, see *Catechism of the Catholic Church*, Part 3, Section 2, Chapter 2, Article 6, online at http://www.vatican.va/archive/ccc_css/archive/catechism/p3s2c2a6.htm.

2. Human decree cannot simply undo what God has done. Some divorces may take place properly in the eyes of the law, but not in reality. This is why Jesus describes remarriage after divorce as adultery. That is, the previous marriage still exists, even if it has been dissolved legally.

3. Marriage is not just a convenient biological mechanism to make babies, nor simply a pragmatic way of protecting relationships. God gave the 'one flesh' union of wife and husband to reflect God's relationship of absolute love for and commitment to God's people. Marriage is a picture of how closely and intimately we are united to Jesus Christ, and of how God never gives up on us, no matter what we do. Divorce is possible, but it is always a tragedy, because it falls short of God's wonderful purpose for marriage: to be a picture of the gospel.

4. The Bible's restrictions on divorce protect the vulnerable, especially women and children. When the Bible was written, women had few rights and little power over their own lives. Divorce could usually only be initiated by men, and often left the woman with children to support and no easy prospect of earning a living. Today, in theory, women have better employment prospects, and we expect fathers to contribute financially to their children's care. But unequal pay is still widespread, and more than 90 per cent of lone parents are women. Overall, women still bear the financial and practical brunt of marital breakdown.

5. By working through the challenges that all marriages face, couples come face to face with their sinfulness and selfishness, and have the opportunity to repent

and find greater freedom from sin. Divorce can be an escape from this hard but necessary path of transformation. (This point should not be misused to encourage anyone to stay with someone who is abusing them. Abuse is not the same as run-of-the-mill selfishness.)

So, divorce is mostly forbidden and criticised in the Bible because it is usually an exploitative practice that favours men, places an unfair burden on women, causes great personal pain, harms children, fails to bear witness to the gospel significance of marriage, and avoids the liberating but costly self-sacrifice that makes us more like Christ. Yet even so, there are times when the Bible permits divorce and remarriage, and we will look at these now.

The Old Testament attitude to divorce

The Old Testament is ambivalent about divorce. For example, Deuteronomy 24:1–4 acknowledges that divorce takes place. But it does not encourage divorce so much as limit the damage after divorce by saying that a divorced woman should not go back to her first husband if she is unlucky enough to get divorced again.

Another key passage is Exodus 21:10–11. It says that if a man has taken a slave as a wife and then wants another wife as well, he may not 'diminish [the first wife's] food, her clothing, or her marital rights [i.e. affection and sex]' (v. 10). If he neglects her in these ways, he must free her without her having to pay money to redeem herself from slavery (v. 11).

But is this passage really about divorce? The point of the law is to protect women who have already been enslaved and married regardless of their wishes from the consequences of polygamy. The outcome for such women is not divorce as such, but freedom from slavery. Again, the purpose was damage limitation.

So, the Old Testament recognises that divorce, slavery and polygamy happen, but that doesn't mean it approves of them. Rather, the Law mitigates them and protects their victims. It's a bit like the Slave Trade Act of 1807. This outlawed the slave trade, but it did not set existing slaves free. That came later. At the time, outlawing the trade was the best that the abolitionists could get, and it was better than nothing. You could even say that in a sense the Act of 1807 continued to allow slavery. But that doesn't mean it was in favour of it. It was just that the Act needed enough political support to pass. Law, like politics, is the art of the possible.

Similarly, the Old Testament divorce laws are damage limitation. If divorce was simply illegal, vulnerable women would be worse off. Some husbands would still abandon their wives, who would remain legally married and therefore unable to marry again. In some societies in the ancient world, the husband could come back and reclaim his wife and children later if it suited him, so other men would be reluctant to marry a divorcee.[8] The Law therefore limits divorce to certain circumstances, so that husbands could

---

[8]See David Instone-Brewer, *Divorce and Remarriage in the Church: Biblical Solutions for Pastoral Realities* (Milton Keynes: Paternoster, 2011), Kindle edition, ch. 2.

not abandon women on a whim or because they wanted a new wife, and the Law requires a husband to give his wife a certificate of divorce so that her freedom to remarry was publicly recognised. In this sense, the Law allows divorce. But that doesn't mean it approves. The intention was to protect the people who had the most to lose. The Law allows divorce, precisely in order to regulate it.

Reasons for divorce in the Old Testament

So, when *does* the Law allow divorce? Exodus 21:11, as we have seen, requires a husband to set his slave wife free without payment if he diminished her 'food, her clothing, or her marital rights'. Some therefore conclude that God allowed divorce if someone deprives their spouse in any of these ways. But remember that the woman in this case is a slave, so the solution to her plight is freedom, not divorce. Also, the point of the law was to protect the first wife in a polygamous marriage from being deprived rather than to set out a general rule for divorce in monogamous marriages. The principle here is that polygamous men must treat all their wives properly, not that divorce may take place when any husband deprives his wife of food, clothing or love.

Going back to Deuteronomy 24:1, divorce was legitimate if the husband 'found some indecency' in his wife. The Hebrew for 'indecency' is *erwat dabar*, which literally means 'a matter (or cause) of nakedness'. This refers to sexual immorality such as adultery or if the wife turns out not to have been a virgin when she got married. If we take it literally, it could even mean a woman being naked in public. So, since I have argued that Exodus 21:11 does not refer to divorce in general, the only time that the Law actually allowed divorce was when a woman had been sexually immoral.[9]

Does God say 'I hate divorce'?

One frequently quoted verse about divorce is Malachi 2:16, which some Bible versions translate as 'I hate divorce.' If they are right, this seems like a 'clobber text', ruling out divorce in general. But this reads more into the text than it says. Whilst it is hardly a ringing endorsement of divorce, it does not say, 'divorce is impossible', or 'divorce should never take place'. The phrase simply expresses God's general feelings about it.

More importantly, the 'clobber' approach rips the verse out of its context. The passage in which it occurs (Mal. 2:13–16) refers to the practice of a man divorcing 'the

---

[9]It is only fair to let readers know that my interpretation differs from a leading authority on this subject, David Instone-Brewer (see his *Divorce and Remarriage in the Church*, ch. 3). He argues that divorce is legitimate for four reasons: failure to provide food, or clothing, lack of conjugal love (including but not only sex), and sexual infidelity. Abuse would also be a legitimate reason for divorce, since it is an extreme version of lack of love. Instone-Brewer suggests that these four grounds for divorce reflect the four marriage vows: to provide food, to provide clothing, to love and to be faithful. He therefore concludes that the Law allows divorce if someone breaks their marriage vows. But the texts themselves make no reference to the marriage vows being broken. And there are very few marriages where there has never been a withdrawal of marital love. Instone-Brewer doesn't want the slippery slope this introduces – but it is not clear to me that he can protect against it.

wife of [his] youth', who has borne his children and given him companionship, so that he can marry somebody else. The emphasis is not on divorce in general, but on divorce springing from unfaithfulness. Once again, the concern is to protect vulnerable and innocent women.

Why is there a difference between the Old Testament Law and the teaching of Jesus?

When quizzed about divorce in Mark 10, Jesus's response seems very hardline: the Old Testament permitted divorce as a concession to the sinfulness of humanity. Divorce does not reflect God's original intention for marriage. For this, Jesus goes back to the creation story in Genesis 2 (i.e. prior to our sin messing things up in Gen. 3). The Law is not sufficient as a moral guide – not because it is legalistic, but because it is too easy.

This brings most of us up sharp. When we read the Law today, its punishments seem severe, even barbaric. This makes the Law seem very fierce. Thankfully, these punishments do not apply in the New Testament. But that does not mean that the New Testament has lower moral standards.[10] In fact, Jesus usually increases the moral demand on his followers rather than relaxing it, because he calls us to live under God's perfect reign here and now. For example, Matthew 5 gives six cases where Jesus quotes an Old Testament Law, but then adds to each quotation an instruction that is more challenging and of a higher

---

[10]See Kevin Scott, *At Variance: The Church's Argument Against Homosexual Conduct* (Edinburgh: Dunedin Academic Press, 2004), p. 29.

standard than the original law, often taking the fight to the deeper issues that underlie our wrong outward deeds. And, of course, the New Testament strongly emphasises the gift of the Holy Spirit, who changes us from within and thus enables us to live this new and demanding way of life, making it something joyful and not oppressive.

In case this sounds like I am writing off the Law (a charge from which Jesus and Paul sometimes also had to defend themselves), let me add that there is a good reason for this. God did not intend the Law to be a full moral guide. It was a legal code for the social and religious life of Israel and therefore made allowances for the fallen reality of that society, as all laws must. Even a God-given law can never express all of what God made us to be. It can prohibit violent deeds, for example, but it cannot address the root causes of violence or change the human heart. Conversely, nobody thinks that inward states such as lust or hatred should be illegal, even though they are immoral. The Law often represents a huge advance on the other cultures of its day, and offered protection to the vulnerable. But it is a *minimum* standard, not an unachievable pinnacle.[11]

Similarly, it is true that some Old Testament commands do not apply to Gentile Christians, such as the food laws and circumcision (see Mark 7:18–19, for example). And we no longer practice the sacrificial system, because Christ has sacrificed himself 'once for all' (Heb. 9 and 10). But that

---

[11]See Gordon J. Wenham, *Story as Torah: Reading the Old Testament Ethically* (Edinburgh: T&T Clark, 2000), ch. 5.

does not mean that Jesus abolished the moral standards of the Old Testament.

The pattern with respect to divorce in Mark 10 (and its parallel in Matt. 19) is very similar. Jesus admits that the Law accepts marital breakdown as a reality in a fallen world. But he attributes this precisely to 'your hardness of heart' (Mark 10:5; Matt.19:8). That is, we are in a situation in which the vulnerable need protecting. The Law restrains and regulates divorce, which is appropriate for a legal code, but not for a full guide to what God actually wants for our lives. Following Jesus is not about getting away with as much as we can whilst staying within the rules, but living a new, Spirit-empowered life. Jesus brings transformation to every area of life, including marriage.

Jesus bases this renewal on the way God originally made us, 'from the beginning of creation' (Mark 10:6). He then quotes from the second creation story: 'Therefore a man shall leave his father and mother and hold fast to his wife, and the two shall become one flesh' (Mark 10:7–8, quoting Genesis 2:24). The fact that God made humanity male and female is the reason that marriage is a monogamous and permanent union of husband and wife whom 'God has joined together' (Mark 10:9). This is why a wife and husband should not 'separate', and why Jesus then describes remarriage after divorce, at least in some cases, as adultery. For Jesus, the reality of the way God originally made us takes precedence over the fact that we are fallen. We see how God really wants us to live by looking not at how things are now but at how God originally made us.

Legitimate divorce 1: sexual immorality

So Jesus had a very strict attitude towards divorce and remarriage. However, he permitted them in certain circumstances. Now we have set out his general teaching against divorce and remarriage, it's time to look at the exceptions.

We saw that the Old Testament permits divorce as a response to sexual impropriety, especially adultery. Matthew explicitly upholds this view. When Joseph finds out that Mary is pregnant (and naturally assumes she has been unfaithful), he intends to 'divorce her quietly' (Matt. 1:19). Far from being criticised for this, Joseph is described as 'just' or 'righteous' for not disgracing her publicly.

Matthew's account of Jesus's teaching says the same thing. If we only had Mark's gospel, we would probably think that Jesus never allowed divorce and remarriage. But in Matthew, Jesus allows at least one exception, which is when 'sexual immorality' (the Greek word is *porneia*) has been committed (Matt. 5:32 and 19:9).

Porneia comes from the word *porne*, which meant 'prostitute'. *Porneia* is therefore a general word for sexual sin, including prostitution (Jas 2:25), incest (1 Cor. 5:1), and adultery.[12] This should sound familiar. Remember, sexual activity outside marriage was the reason that Deuteronomy 24:1 permitted divorce. If a spouse is sexually unfaithful, they have damaged the 'one flesh' nature of the marriage

---

[12]For a technical analysis of the term, see Kyle Harper, '*Porneia*: The Making of a Christian Sexual Norm' in *Journal of Biblical Literature*, 131.2 (2011), pp. 363–383.

in such a profound way that the victim may divorce them and remarry.

Divorce in such circumstances is not compulsory. God delights in bringing about repentance and reconciliation. Leaping into divorce too quickly might forego an opportunity for God-given restoration. But other times the trust and bond of marriage are damaged irrevocably, hence the victim of adultery is not sinning by initiating a divorce.

So why is there a difference between Mark and Matthew? Mark wrote before Matthew, and Matthew used Mark as a basis for his own gospel. So, if Matthew used Mark's account of Jesus's teaching on divorce, why did he add the words 'except *porneia*', where previously no exceptions were allowed to the prohibition of divorce? One explanation is that Matthew is toning down Mark's supposedly overly strict teaching. I don't find this convincing, because Matthew is first in the queue when it comes to pointing out when the standards of the Law are too weak.

The answer to the conundrum is in the question the Pharisees ask Jesus in Matthew 19:3: 'Is it lawful to divorce one's wife *for any cause*?' Matthew has also added the phrase 'for any cause' (see Mark 10:2). This reflects a heated debate between two then-prominent rabbis, Hillel and Shammai.

Shammai tended to be stricter than Hillel. For example, Hillel permitted white lies and Shammai did not. When it came to Deuteronomy 24:1, which permitted divorce if someone found 'indecency' in his wife, Shammai thought that 'indecency' meant only sexual indecency, especially adultery, whilst Hillel argued that 'indecency' meant anything displeasing about her, including spoiling the dinner. In other words, Hillel permitted divorce 'for any cause'. Both agreed that divorce could take place if either party withdrew food, clothing, or conjugal love (because of Exod. 21:10–11).

So, when the Pharisees in Mark 10:2 asked Jesus whether divorce was lawful, they were not asking him a general question. They were asking him *where he stood in this debate*. They had no need to say 'for any cause', because everyone agreed that divorce was lawful. The question was whether it was lawful for any reason or not. And when Jesus said it was not lawful, he had no need to add 'except for adultery', because everyone knew that was lawful. If someone asks, 'Do you drink?' we know they mean, 'Do you drink alcohol?' Or, if a man asks his wife, 'Shall I wear a jacket over this shirt?' and she replies, 'Just wear the shirt,' she would be shocked if he did not put on any trousers![13]

Mark simply records the words more or less as they were spoken. Everyone knew that divorce for sexual immorality was acceptable, so he doesn't need to spell this out. But Matthew, writing later on, adds 'for any cause' and 'except for sexual immorality' to clarify what Jesus originally meant, namely that you can't get divorced 'for any cause', but only for *porneia*.

---

[13]These examples are adapted from David Instone-Brewer, *Divorce and Remarriage in the Church*, ch. 5.

Jesus was often counter-cultural. Here he is being even stricter than the already-strict Shammai.[14] Jesus allows divorce after sexual immorality, but he does not mention withdrawal of food, clothing or love (not surprising given that Exod. 21 isn't really about divorce). His words in Matthew 5:31–32 corroborate this. There, Jesus is not responding to a question about Hillelite 'any cause' divorce, so his words cannot refer to that. Instead, it is a *general* prohibition of divorce, the only exception to which is *porneia*. Clearly, Jesus is normally opposed to divorce, with the exception of when sexual immorality (primarily adultery) has taken place. Adultery violates the 'one flesh' nature of marriage so deeply that divorce does not initiate marital break-up so much as recognize that break-up has already happened.

Legitimate divorce 2: being unwillingly divorced

Earlier, I quoted 1 Corinthians 7:10–11, where Paul states his general view (based on Jesus's teaching), that married couples should not 'separate'. If they have, they should either seek reconciliation or, if this is not possible, remain unmarried.

The reason Paul uses the word 'separate' is that, in the Greco-Roman context of Corinth, divorce happened simply

---

[14]This is evident in the fact that Jesus astonishes his disciples by what he says, so that they almost renounce marriage: 'If such is the case of a man with his wife, it is better not to marry' (Matt. 19:10). It's unlikely that they would be so surprised if Jesus was just advocating one of the standard views of the day.

by the couple separating. This is evident in what Paul says next: 'If any brother has a wife who is an unbeliever, and she consents to live with him, he should not divorce her. If any woman has a husband who is an unbeliever, and he consents to live with her, she should not divorce him' (vv. 12–13). What is decisive is 'living with', because divorce happened through separation. In other words, divorce was extremely easy.

Whilst Christians shouldn't initiate divorce, Paul adds that 'if the unbelieving partner separates, let it be so' (v. 15). A Christian should not initiate a separation just because they are married to a non-Christian. But if the non-Christian leaves, let them, so that you can live 'at peace' with others. You don't need to try to make them stay. When a non-Christian divorces a Christian, the Christian is 'not enslaved' (v. 15). (The next section explains why this means that they are free to remarry.)

But what if a Christian is divorced by another Christian? I think they are also free to remarry. For Paul, the fact that one spouse is a Christian and one is not does not soften the marriage bond. What destroys the bond in Paul's example must be the divorce itself.

So, whilst nobody should initiate divorce unless adultery has taken place, people who have been divorced against their will have done nothing wrong and are free to remarry. Similarly, they are not obliged to oppose a divorce petition (although, of course, they may have good reasons for doing so) because Paul says, 'Let it be so . . . God has called you to peace' (v. 15). This is important today because it could mean the difference between having to wait two years after separation rather than five.

When can a divorcee get remarried?

So, we have seen that Jesus allowed people to initiate divorce for adultery, and Paul says that someone who has been divorced by their spouse is 'not enslaved' (1 Cor. 7:15). Does this mean that the victims of divorce and adultery may remarry, or simply that they are not obliged to try to maintain their previous marriage?

One view is that, because Jesus describes remarriage after divorce as adultery, real divorce is never possible: marriage is indissoluble. The original couple is still one flesh, even if they are living separately and indeed even if they have remarried. When Jesus permitted divorce after adultery, he meant only separation 'from bed and board', in Augustine's phrase. This view can also appeal to 1 Corinthians 7:11: 'she should remain unmarried or else be reconciled to her husband'.

I do not find this view persuasive, as 1 Corinthians 7:11 is addressed to people who have initiated divorce, not to its victims. And, as we have seen, Matthew 19:9 describes remarriage after divorce as adultery *except* when it follows sexual immorality. The implication is that remarriage after sexual immorality is not adultery, which must mean that the original marriage has truly ended. But most importantly, in Jesus's context, divorce meant by definition that you could marry again. The Jewish divorce certificate said simply, 'You are free to marry any [Jewish] man you wish.'[15] By permitting divorce after adultery, Jesus permitted remarriage too.

Similarly, the phrase, 'not enslaved' in 1 Corinthians 7:15 must mean, 'free to remarry'. Under Roman law, you obtained the freedom to remarry simply by separating from your previous spouse. This is corroborated by the fact that Paul uses the same word in verses 27 and 39 to say wife and husband are 'bound' together, which he contrasts with being 'free' to marry (see also Rom. 7:2–3). Not being bound means being able to marry. So, Paul permits a victim of divorce to remarry, but not the initiator of the divorce (1Cor. 7–11) (although I find Instone-Brewer's argument convincing that even the latter could remarry if their original spouse does, i.e. once reconciliation is no longer possible).[16]

Is there a contradiction between the teachings of Jesus and Paul?

It might look like it. Jesus says that we should never initiate divorce, except after adultery. But Paul allows remarriage if a non-Christian leaves a Christian. Isn't this a second reason for divorce?

I don't think this is a contradiction, for the simple reason that Jesus speaks of when someone can rightly *initiate* divorce, whereas Paul is saying that you can remarry when someone has *already divorced you.*

---

[15]*Divorce and Remarriage in the Church*, ch. 2.
[16]*Divorce and Remarriage in the Church*, ch. 9.

Violence and abuse[17]

I have argued that, according to Jesus, someone can only legitimately initiate divorce when their spouse has committed adultery, that nobody is obliged to resist divorce, and that someone who has been divorced or has initiated divorce following adultery is free to remarry.

But there are other situations when it is difficult or dangerous for a couple to remain together. The most obvious example is abuse. Abuse takes many forms. Physical abuse may include pushing someone, pulling their hair, preventing them from taking medication, restricting their freedom, damaging their property or exhausting them. Emotional abuse may include humiliating someone, preventing someone from maintaining good relationships with friends and family, name-calling, constant criticism, and making threats. It may be sexual, such as forcing someone to do sexual acts, rejecting them sexually, or interfering with contraception. It can be financial: preventing someone from working (or forcing them to work), controlling the finances, or expecting someone to account for every penny.

Research estimates that one in four women suffer abuse from a partner. Two women a week are killed by their partners or former partners, and more die by suicide to escape abuse.[18] Of course, men can also experience abuse. And there are other behaviours that are extremely hurtful and difficult to live with too, such as

---

[17]I am very grateful to Natalie Collins of Spark for her generous help with this section. See http://www.sparkequip.org/.

[18]See http://www.refuge.org.uk/.

financial irresponsibility, addiction, and someone ceasing to show any interest in or love towards a spouse. In such cases, it seems unfair to us today, and in some circumstances very dangerous, that anyone should remain trapped in such marriages.

Someone who is being hurt and/or controlled by their partner should not hesitate to get appropriate outside support, including the police where relevant (including co-operating with any investigation and prosecution).[19] Some Christians may hold back from involving the police, because of Jesus's teaching that they should turn the other cheek. Of course, they are correct not to respond violently, although they may need to act in self-defence or to defend their children.[20] But domestic violence is not a private matter. It is a crime. We must read 'turn the other cheek' alongside passages such as Romans 13, which says that God has established the governing authorities to deter and punish wrongdoing. The Bible speaks frequently of God's care for the vulnerable and victimised, which is precisely why God gives civil government. The weak should therefore certainly seek help from the (admittedly imperfect) institutions that God has made to

---

[19]The 24 Hour National Domestic Violence Helpline on 0808 2000 247 provides information about such support, and see www.womensaid. org.uk and http://www.refuge.org.uk/. See also Restored, a Christian alliance seeking to end violence against women: http://www.restore-drelationships.org/.

[20]Where children are involved, church members and leaders must obviously follow proper safeguarding policies, which will invariably include reporting concerns to the proper authorities.

protect them. It is important to remember this because, usually, abusive spouses are highly manipulative and act in a sorrowful way to try to persuade their victim to stay with them.

If the perpetrator is not removed or willing to leave whilst they get professional help, the person experiencing abuse should not hesitate to leave the marital home (and take any children with them). This is for their safety but, in a sense, this is also helping the abusive partner by hopefully depriving him (or her) of further opportunities to commit very serious sins. If a woman experiencing abuse chooses to leave, she is very likely to need support and help to do so, because trying to leave can actually make things more dangerous for her.

The person who is being hurt may feel obliged to stick by their spouse and be faithful to their marriage. But as well as teaching against divorce and remarriage, Jesus also teaches on dealing openly with sin:

> If your brother sins against you, go and tell him his fault, between you and him alone. If he listens to you, you have gained your brother. But if he does not listen, take one or two others along with you, that every charge may be established by the evidence of two or three witnesses. If he refuses to listen to them, tell it to the church. And if he refuses to listen even to the church, let him be to you as a Gentile and a tax collector.
>
> *Matthew 18:15–17*

So turning the other cheek does not mean ignoring wrongdoing or allowing people to mistreat you. It means handling wrongdoing the right way, which may well include involving others. For Jesus, confrontation needs community. So, someone who is experiencing abuse need not feel guilty or disloyal about involving other people by getting help. Whatever else has happened, abuse is always the responsibility of the perpetrator and never the fault of the victim.

Church members and leaders must listen to and take seriously any claim of abuse, and must involve specialist domestic abuse services immediately.[21] Whatever someone has disclosed is likely to be the tip of the iceberg, and many perpetrators will try to co-opt church leaders and members as allies. The purpose of abuse is to gain power and control over someone, and so our role involves empowering the person who has been hurt. Too often the church has colluded with or covered up abuse, whereas Jesus teaches that those who refuse to repent of their sin must be exposed. (Not that church leaders should confront the abuser themselves, as this is likely to put the person suffering abuse at risk.)

Expressions of sorrow and promises not to do it again are not enough. Repentance is not simply remorse. It includes taking concrete steps to put it right, such as leaving the marital home whilst they engage fully with any criminal processes and get proper help to change their

---

[21]See footnote 20 for details. Also see *Ending Domestic Abuse*, a useful pack for churches produced by Restored, online at: http://www.restoredrelationships.org/resources/info/51/.

behaviour.[22] If they are not willing to take such steps, they are not really acknowledging the seriousness of their crime and sin. That is, they are not yet repentant. A good biblical example here is Joseph in Genesis 44. Rather than seeking reconciliation immediately, Joseph first tests his brothers to see if they have changed. His goal is still reconciliation, but reconciliation (unlike forgiveness) requires true repentance on the part of the wrongdoer.

If there is no repentance and restitution, ultimately the Christian fellowship must exclude the perpetrator. In other words, there is a genuine basis in Jesus's teaching for a victim to separate from the perpetrator. The purpose of discipline is not to punish someone, but to show them the serious consequences of their unwillingness to repent. The hope is that showing them what God must eventually do to them if they do not repent will bring them to repentance (1 Cor. 5:5). Separation here is not judgement or punishment, but love.

But is someone obliged to remain married to someone who has abused them, or could abuse be a legitimate reason for divorce? The best way to argue for this would be by analogy with adultery. Jesus allowed divorce and remarriage following adultery, because adultery is such a

---

[22]That is, accessing an accredited perpetrator programme. Counselling, anger management, addiction treatment, pastoral care and/or marriage courses are all helpful in other circumstances, but are not adequate programmes for perpetrators of domestic abuse. For information on such programmes, call Respect on 0808 802 4040 or see http://www.respectphoneline.org.uk/pages/domestic-violence-prevention-programmes.html.

profound violation of marriage that it effectively renders the marriage over (unless the victim chooses to forgive). So you could argue that Jesus would also allow divorce for abuse, which is an equivalent kind of violation to adultery.

However, although I have said that it is essential to leave a dangerous situation, to seek professional help, and to separate permanently if the perpetrator of abuse does not repent, I have to say that I cannot see a biblical basis for initiating divorce in such circumstances. Jesus only gave one exception to his prohibition of divorce and I don't think we can add to that. I am very aware that this conclusion will seem very unfair to some, and of course other theologians have reached different conclusions.[23] All I would ask is that if you do reach a different point of view, you do so on the basis of the Bible.

If someone wrongly initiated a divorce, should they try to return to their first marriage?

If neither party has remarried and both are willing, reconciliation can be wonderful – although some good relationship counselling and support will almost certainly be needed. If you initiated a divorce that you now believe was wrong, but your ex-spouse is not willing to try reconciliation, I think you should probably stay single, unless they remarry. But if either or both of you have remarried, then your previous marriage certainly has ended, even if the original marriage was not broken by the legal divorce. If so, whilst you repent

[23]For example, see Barbara Roberts, *Not Under Bondage: Biblical Divorce for Abuse, Adultery and Desertion* (Australia: Maschil Press, 2008), ch. 3.

of what you have done and seek to put it right in other ways, don't break up your new marriage in order to return to an original one. Two wrongs don't make a right!

Should divorcees remarry in church?

Churches have to make some very tough calls when approached by couples who wish to remarry in church. Many will be faithful church members, whom the church already cares for personally. Others may not be Christians at all, and the church will rightly want them to feel accepted and loved, so that they may discover Jesus for themselves.

Some churches and ministers refuse to conduct marriages if people are divorced and their ex-spouse is still living, because Jesus describes remarriage as being adultery in most circumstances. Even though divorce has legally taken place, the original couple is still married. This approach is rightly cautious of sanctioning adultery, but it ignores the fact that the Bible allows remarriage after divorce in some circumstances.

At the opposite extreme, other churches allow anyone to be remarried, because it is up to the couple to decide whether or not their marriage is right in the sight of God. This is somewhat naïve. Yes, we should show everyone God's grace. But forgiveness does not abolish the consequences of what we have done, and one consequence of getting married is that you cannot usually become unmarried. A minister who prevents a couple from entering into what Jesus describes as an adulterous relationship is being kind and not judgemental.

The advantage of both these extremes is that the church (or minister) does not act as judge and jury over individual cases. Churches are neither resourced nor trained to investigate and apportion blame for marital break-ups. However, conducting weddings means you are already involved in the messiness of life. So, I would conduct the wedding of a divorcee where their previous spouse had committed adultery, where they had been divorced against their wishes, or where their previous spouse had already remarried. The crucial factor in each of these cases is that the previous marriage has genuinely ended, and that the new marriage cannot therefore be adultery. In some situations, I might speak to their former spouse, to hear their side of the story, and explore gently what steps the person had taken since the break-up of their first marriage to seek reconciliation, and how they had learned and grown from the experience.[24] Phrases that ring alarm bells are, 'The marriage didn't work' or 'We drifted apart'. This suggests that there is some third quantity in between the two partners that is at fault, whereas according to the Bible a marriage cannot end itself, but only through the actions of one of the parties. Ministers often have to make tricky judgements and will not always get it right.

Conclusion

Jesus calls us to live according to the way God originally made us. Marriage was created by God to be a lifelong

---

[24]Obviously, there would be times when this would not be appropriate – as in the case of abuse.

union between a woman and a man that reflects God's relationship with his people. That's why you cannot leave a marriage in the same way you entered it, namely by making a decision. But marriage *can* be dissolved by the actions of the other person – either adultery/sexual unfaithfulness or by them initiating divorce. So no one should initiate divorce, except for adultery, but neither is anyone obliged to contest a divorce. A victim of divorce or adultery is free to remarry, as is someone whose previous spouse has remarried.

According to Jesus, remarriage after divorce is often adultery because the previous marriage still exists. So, approach remarriage with caution. Only remarry if you are sure that the previous marriage is over (i.e. because your previous spouse committed adultery, because they initiated the divorce or because they have since remarried).

Reconciliation and restoration are wonderful, but not always possible – for example, when an abusive person professes repentance but is unwilling to make amends and seek proper help. Although I do not think domestic abuse of itself makes it right to initiate a divorce, a person experiencing abuse is not obliged to stay with their spouse. I know this is asking something incredibly difficult, but it does seem to me that adultery is the only time that Jesus allowed someone to initiate divorce.

Marriage isn't easy (but then neither is singleness). But it is a beautiful gift that God has given to humanity to show us something of who God is. For those who are married, it also has the potential to be a place in which another person confronts and knows us at our deepest level, yet loves and accepts us for who we are. That is profoundly life-changing and transforming. Yet precisely because of its depth, marriage is deeply risky and therefore devastating when it falls apart. I hope I have challenged you to stick with and/or support marriage, but also encouraged you with a fresh sense of the security that God bestows on it. After all, it is God who joins people together. So, ultimately and thankfully, the success of marriage does not depend on us.

Go Deeper

Andrew Cornes, *Divorce and Remarriage: Biblical Principles and Pastoral Practice* (Tain: Christian Focus, 2002).

David Instone-Brewer, *Divorce and Remarriage in the Church: Biblical Solutions for Pastoral Realities* (Milton Keynes: Paternoster, 2011).

Barbara Roberts, *Not Under Bondage: Biblical Divorce for Abuse, Adultery and Desertion* (Australia: Maschil Press, 2008).

Mark L. Strauss (ed.), *Remarriage After Divorce in Today's Church: Three Views* (Grand Rapids, MI: Zondervan, 2006).